D0539951

Emergence of the Psychic

Governance of Life by the Soul

Selections from the Works of
SRI AUROBINDO
and
THE MOTHER

Compiled with an Introduction by
A. S. Dalal

SRI AUROBINDO ASHRAM
PONDICHERRY

First edition 2002
Third impression 2016

Rs 65
ISBN 978-81-7058-688-3

© Sri Aurobindo Ashram Trust 2002
Published by Sri Aurobindo Ashram Publication Department
Pondicherry 605 002
Web http://www.sabda.in

Printed at Sri Aurobindo Ashram Press, Pondicherry
PRINTED IN INDIA

CONTENTS

The soul, the psychic being is in direct touch with the divine Truth, but it is hidden in man by the mind, the vital being and the physical nature. One may practise yoga and get illuminations in the mind and the reason; one may conquer power and luxuriate in all kinds of experiences in the vital; one may establish even surprising physical Siddhis; but if the true soul-power behind does not manifest, if the psychic nature does not come into the front, nothing genuine has been done.* ...Mind can open by itself to its own higher reaches; it can still itself and widen into the Impersonal; it may too spiritualise itself in some kind of static liberation or Nirvana; but the supramental cannot find a sufficient base in a spiritualised mind alone.

SRI AUROBINDO

(*Letters on Yoga*, Sri Aurobindo Birth Centenary Library,
Vol. 24, p. 1095)

---

* From the viewpoint of transformation, conceived as a goal beyond liberation. (Ed.)

We give the name "psychic" to the psychological centre of our being, the seat within us of the highest truth of our existence, that which can know this truth and set it in movement. It is therefore of capital importance to become conscious of its presence in us, to concentrate on this presence until it becomes a living fact for us and we can identify ourselves with it.

THE MOTHER

(*On Education*, Collected Works of the Mother, Vol. 12, p. 4)

*

Is identification with the psychic the same thing as the psychic coming in front?

That is, the first step is the identification, and then, once you can keep this identification, the psychic governs the rest of the nature and life. It becomes the master of existence. So this is what we mean by the psychic coming in front. It is that which governs, directs, even organises the life, organises the consciousness, the different parts of the being. When this happens, the work goes very fast. Very fast, well...relatively very fast.

THE MOTHER

Questions and Answers 1954, Collected Works of the Mother,
Vol. 6, p. 334)

FOREWORD

The two basic concepts of the Vedanta are the all-pervasive Divine — the Brahman — and the spark or reflection of this Divine within each being, specially human beings — the Atman, and joining these two — Yoga — is the well-established methodology to be found in our scriptures and in the teachings of realised seers and saints down through the millennia. Within this broad Brahman-Atman-Yoga framework, there are an infinite number of possibilities, theories and practices flowing from the essential pluralistic nature of Hinduism which accepts multiple paths to the Divine — *ekaṁ sad viprā bahudhā vadanti* — as the Rigveda has it. Down through the ages, our sacred texts have been reinterpreted and rearticulated by a whole series of self-realised souls.

In the 20th century itself, which has just drawn to a close, we have had outstanding figures such as Swami Vivekananda, Sri Ramana Maharshi, Sri Aurobindo and the Mother, Sri Krishna Prem and a number of other men and women who, through the dint of their *sādhanā* and realisation have re-illuminated the path to the Divine. Sri Aurobindo in particular, with his outstanding intellect, magnificent power of expression and deep yogic attainments, has in his voluminous writings thrown tremendous light upon the whole process of spiritual development.

We speak rather loosely of the 'soul', but Sri Aurobindo has clearly explored and articulated for us the various levels or degrees of inner consciousness, and the methodologies whereby we can grow towards the Divine. In his formulation, the key concept is of what he calls the 'Psychic Being'.

As he defines it:

> What is meant in the terminology of the yoga by the psychic
> is the soul element in the nature, the pure psychic or divine
> nucleus which stands behind mind, life and body (it is not
> the ego) but of which we are only dimly aware. It is a
> portion of the Divine and permanent from life to life, tak-
> ing the experience of life through its outer instruments.
> As this experience grows it manifests a developing psy-
> chic personality which insisting always on the good, true
> and beautiful, finally becomes ready and strong enough
> to turn the nature towards the Divine. It can then come
> entirely forward, breaking through the mental, vital and
> physical screen, govern the instincts and transform the
> nature. Nature no longer imposes itself on the soul, but
> the soul, the Purusha, imposes its dictates on the nature.

He also adds:

> The psychic being is quite different from the mind or vital;
> it stands behind them where they meet in the heart. Its
> central place is there, but behind the heart rather than in
> the heart; for what men call usually the heart is the seat of
> emotion, and human emotions are mental-vital impulses,
> not ordinarily psychic in their nature. This mostly secret
> power behind, other than the mind and the life-force, is the
> true soul, the psychic being in us. The power of the psychic,
> however, can act upon the mind and vital and body,
> purifying thought and perception and emotion (which then
> becomes psychic feeling) and sensation and action and

everything else in us and preparing them to be divine movements.

Shri A.S. Dalal has, over the last several years, produced a series of excellent selections from the writings of Sri Aurobindo and the Mother on a whole variety of spiritual concepts. In this book — *Emergence of the Psychic* — he has once again produced for us an excellent selection of writings by Sri Aurobindo and the Mother on this whole concept of the psychic being, its emergence from the mass of inertia under which it lies buried, and its ultimate role as the direct link with the Divine. This flows from Sri Aurobindo's remarkable theory of spiritual evolution, according to which, although every individual has a spark of the Divine, it is only when the spark becomes individualised that it emerges as the Psychic Being which then, if recognized and accepted by our physical, emotional and mental consciousness, evolves into a direct contact with the Godhead. As the Mother writes:

> It is this spark that is permanent and gathers round itself all sorts of elements for the formation of that individuality; the true psychic being is formed only when the psychic personality is fully grown, fully built up, round the eternal divine spark; it attains its culmination, its total fulfilment if and when it unites with a being or personality from above.

What is particularly interesting is the way in which the Mother amplifies and explains in simpler language the great concepts articulated by Sri Aurobindo, which in turn flow from his exalted spiritual stature. Spiritual seekers around the world, whether or not they are formally following Sri Aurobindo's Integral Yoga, will find this selection of great value in their quest. I myself have benefited greatly from Shri Dalal's earlier selections, and warmly commend the valuable service that he is rendering to genuine seekers for the Divine.

KARAN SINGH
15 August 2002

PREFACE

This book aims at three main objectives. First, it is meant to help one in becoming more conscious of what most human beings are almost entirely unconscious, namely, the action and influence of the soul in one's life.

Secondly, the book seeks to describe and clarify various states of consciousness that pertain to experiences of the soul. These include the influence of the psychic, coming in contact or being in touch with the psychic, discovery of, identification with or awakening of the psychic, and the opening, coming forward or emergence of the psychic. Such a clarification provides a mental understanding that can be helpful not only in conceiving and distinguishing the various experiences of the psychic but also in becoming aware more readily of the moments when one is or is not under the influence of the psychic or in contact with it. By learning to recognise the presence or absence of the psychic consciousness, one is apt to grow more conscious of the factors which are helpful and those which are harmful in fostering the awareness of one's soul. This, in turn, enables one to adopt attitudes and make choices in one's life that are more conducive to the consciousness of the psychic.

Thirdly, and most importantly, the book aims at kindling an aspiration for a spiritual goal which goes beyond the discovery and freedom of the soul — one which envisages the governance of life and the transformation of one's outer being by the soul.

This book is in a way an expansion on a previous compilation, *The Psychic Being — Soul: Its Nature, Mission and*

Evolution, which dealt with the basic theoretical and practical aspects of the subject. The present compilation deals much more extensively with the practical aspects. In order that this book can be read independently, it does include a few passages that can be found also in the earlier book.

Some of the ideas contained in this book have been inspiringly expressed in various passages of Sri Aurobindo's epic, *Savitri*. Such passages will be found in the Appendix at the end of the book.

I wish to express my deep gratitude to Dr. Karan Singh for his kind Foreword in which he has so effectively introduced Sri Aurobindo's paramount but relatively less familiar concept of the psychic being.

A. S. D.

INTRODUCTION

One of the most inspiring and ennobling concepts in the spiritual lore of the world is that of the psychic being. It provides a major key for understanding the significance and process of the evolution of consciousness, and offers a potent tool for the transformation of consciousness. The concept of the psychic thus ranks among the outstanding contributions made by yogic experience to psychological thought and spiritual practice.

What is the Psychic?

Sri Aurobindo, who uses the term "psychic" for what is popularly and often vaguely called the soul, distinguishes between the *psychic principle*, which is present in all things and creatures, and the *psychic personality* which is characteristic of the human state of development. The psychic principle, also referred to variously as psychic essence, psychic existence, soul element, soul-spark, psychic entity or the psyche, is a non-individualised portion of the Divine Consciousness that descends into the evolution "to support the evolution of the individual out of the Ignorance into the Light".[1] It is "the nucleus pregnant with divine possibilities that supports this lower triple manifestation of mind, life and body."[2] In the course of evolution, the psychic principle

---

1. Sri Aurobindo, *Letters on Yoga*, SABCL Vol. 22, p. 295.
2. *Ibid.*, p. 288.

develops in the human being a psychic personality or soul individuality which is called the psychic being. Whereas the psychic principle is immutable and fundamentally always the same, the psychic being is progressive; it grows from life to life, using mind, vital and body as its instruments.[3]

> "The psychic being at its origin is only a spark of the divine consciousness and it is through successive lives that it builds up a conscious individuality. It is a progress similar to that of a growing child. It is a thing in the making. For a long time, in most human beings the psychic is a being in the making. It is not a fully individualised, fully conscious being and master of itself and it needs all its rebirths, one after another, in order to build itself and become fully conscious." (p. 63)

The term "soul" as used in this book generally refers to the non-individualised psychic essence, but sometimes also to the soul individuality or psychic being. Similarly "the psychic" usually means the psychic being but sometimes refers to the psychic essence.

The significance of the psychic being in the evolution of consciousness lies in the fact that the psychic being is "a projection of the divine Consciousness into Matter to awaken Matter out of its inertia so that it takes the path back to the Divine." (p. 11)

3. Mind is generally regarded as the characteristic feature which distinguishes the human being from the animal. But a more salient characteristic distinguishing the human being from the animal is the possession of the psychic being.

The psychic is the psychological centre of our being because it is the inmost part of our being, supporting all other parts—mental, vital, physical. Though in theory the psychic is the true master of the being who puts forth and uses the instruments of mind, life and body, in actuality in most human beings the psychic is entirely veiled and overshadowed by its mental, vital and physical instruments. The outer consciousness of the human being "lives amongst all the external noises and movements in what it sees, what it does, what it says, instead of looking within, into the depths of the being and listening to the inner inspirations" (p. 42). So the psychic being remains behind the outer consciousness as a "secret witness", "a secluded King in a screened chamber", and only a

"constitutional ruler who allows his ministers to rule for him, delegates to them his empire, silently assents to their decisions and only now and then puts in a word which they can at any moment override and act otherwise." (p. 81)

"For the psychic part within is there to support the natural evolution, and the first natural evolution must be the development of body, life and mind, successively, and these must act each in its own kind or together in their ill-assorted partnership in order to grow and have experience and evolve. The soul gathers the essence of all our mental, vital and bodily experience and assimilates it for the farther evolution of our existence in Nature; but this action is occult and not obtruded on the surface." (p. 3)

In most human beings, generally the actual governor or leader who drives one is the vital, for

> "man usually lives in his vital and the body is its instrument and the mind its counsellor and minister (except for the few mental men who live mostly for the things of the mind, but even they are in subjection to the vital in their ordinary movements)." (p. 88)

Because of the fact that the psychic is veiled by and identified with its instruments, most human beings are almost totally unconscious of their psychic being.

> "In the ordinary life there's not one person in a million who has a conscious contact with his psychic being, even momentarily. The psychic being may work from within, but so invisibly and unconsciously for the outer being that it is as though it did not exist. And in most cases, the immense majority, almost the totality of cases, it's as though it were asleep, not at all active, in a kind of torpor." (p. 48)

Therefore, in most human beings the psychic being acts as an unconscious influence rather than as a conscious Presence.

However, though covered over and dominated by mind, vital and physical, the psychic fire is never extinguished by them, for the psychic being is the eternal self "that carries the consciousness from life to life" (p. 16). It is the true and persistent individual whereas our normal self made up of mind, vital and body is only a passing shadow of the true individual.

Nor is the psychic being tarnished by the defects and impurities of the mental, the vital and the physical. For

"It is an ever-pure flame of the divinity in things and nothing that comes to it, nothing that enters into our experience can pollute its purity or extinguish the flame. This spiritual stuff is immaculate and luminous and, because it is perfectly luminous, it is immediately, intimately, directly aware of truth of being and truth of nature; it is deeply conscious of truth and good and beauty because truth and good and beauty are akin to its own native character, forms of something that is inherent in its own substance." (p. 2)

What gets mixed with and contaminated by the mental, vital and physical defects is not the psychic being itself but the action of the psychic being as it comes up from the depths to the surface of the being. It is only as the psychic being emerges more and more in front that it gets clear of the distorting mental, vital and physical mixture.

Influence of the Psychic

Though the psychic in most human beings is entirely veiled so that one is conscious of oneself only as a mental, vital and physical being, there is always an unconscious influence of the psychic even in ordinary life.

"A certain sensitive feeling for all that is true and good
and beautiful, fine and pure and noble, a response to it, a
demand for it, a pressure on mind and life to accept and
formulate it in our thought, feelings, conduct, character
is the most usually recognised, the most general and characteristic, though not the sole sign of this influence of the
psyche. Of the man who has not this element in him or
does not respond at all to this urge, we say that he has no
soul." (p. 30)

"Wherever…there is a spontaneous admiration for the
true, the beautiful, the noble, there is something divine
expressed. You should know for certain that it is the psychic being, the soul in you with which your physical consciousness comes in contact when your heart leaps out to
worship and admire what you feel to be of a divine origin." (p. 21)

Another sign of the influence of the psychic which can be
more readily recognised in human life is the aspiration and
will for progress, for the psychic is the seat and source of all
aspiration for progress.

"Fundamentally, without this kind of inner will of the
psychic being, I believe human beings would be quite
dismal, dull, they would have an altogether animal life.
Every gleam of aspiration is always the expression of a
psychic influence. Without the presence of the psychic,
without the psychic influence, there would never be any
sense of progress or any will for progress." (p. 34)

Faith[4], too, indicates the influence of the psychic. Like aspiration, faith comes from the psychic being, though it may manifest itself in the mind, the vital or even the physical. Similarly, qualities such as goodwill, generosity, love, gratitude and the like, which take one out of one's egoistic self, spring from and express the influence of the psychic.

The soul element in the psychic influence cannot be easily distinguished when it manifests in our mind, vital or physical because when the psychic influence comes up to the surface, an action of the inner being (inner mind, inner vital, inner physical) mixes with and

"distorts or diminishes its self-expression, even causes it to deviate and stumble or stains it with the impurity, smallness and error of mind and life and body; ...a formation of consciousness is accordingly made which is a mixture of the psychic influence and its intimations jumbled with mental ideas and opinions, vital desires and urges, habitual physical tendencies." (p. 31)

Therefore the mind does not generally recognise the deeper nature of the influences which come from the soul;

"our mind does not detect their source; it takes them for its own activities because, before even they come to the surface, they are clothed in mental substance: thus ignorant of their authority, it follows or does not follow them

4. From the viewpoint of yoga, true faith is not a mental belief but a dynamic intuitive conviction in the soul about something for which there is no outward proof.

according to its bent or turn at the moment." (pp. 2-3)

Thus, though the psychic always exerts an influence on our mental, vital and physical being, the influence is almost always hidden, and is not seen or felt.

The psychic exerts an unconscious influence even on the outer circumstances of life, for it is the psychic which guides a human by organising the outer life.

> "If one is very attentive, one becomes aware of it. For instance, when they have decided, in their outer ignorance, to do something, and instead of their being able to do it, all the circumstances are so organised that they do something else, they start shouting.... While most of the time it is just the very circumstance which was most favourable for their inner development.... And when you are a little awake and look back, if you are in the least sincere, you say: 'Ah! It wasn't I who was right—it was Nature or the divine Grace or my psychic being who did it.' "[5]

As the psychic being grows more and more, its action becomes stronger and as a result of its influence all events in life seem to conspire to help one advance on the path. For the psychic being

> "can draw towards you things which help you, draw people, books, circumstances, all sorts of little coincidences which come to you as though brought by some benevo-

5. The Mother, *Questions and Answers 1953*, Collected Works of the Mother, Vol. 5, pp. 394-95.

lent will and give you an indication, a help, a support to take decisions and turn you in the right direction." (p. 38)

When the psychic being has reached a certain stage of its growth, it exerts also a pre-natal influence; "it decides — generally at the last minute of the life it has just finished upon earth — the conditions in which its next life will be passed" (p. 68) and what will be the field of experience in the next life. At an advanced stage of its growth the psychic has the power to influence even the formation of the body in the new life.

"When it has become an almost completely formed and already very conscious being, it presides over the formation of the new body, and usually through an inner influence it chooses the elements and the substance which will form its body in such a way that the body is adapted to the needs of its new experience." (p. 71)

In the case of persons who have reached such an advanced stage, the "psychic being watches over their formation before their birth, even before they are in the womb of their mother."[6]

Contact with the Psychic

Contact with the psychic, like the influence of the psychic, is at first unconscious. An unconscious contact with one's

6. The Mother, *Questions and Answers '50-'51*, Collected Works of the Mother, Vol. 4, p. 140.

psychic being may begin at the moment an infant utters its first cry, but conscious contact with the psychic usually develops only through sadhana, by learning to turn the consciousness within and learning to live within instead of being absorbed in the ordinary surface consciousness. At first and for a long time the contact is only occasional and momentary, followed by lapses into the ordinary consciousness. With the growth of consciousness, the contacts with the psychic become more and more frequent and last longer.

Very often what one comes in contact with is not the psychic being but some part of the mind or the higher vital (emotional) being which is under the influence of the psychic.

"...people enter into contact with these parts and this gives them illuminations, great joy, revelations, and they feel they have found their soul. But it is only the part of the being under its influence, one part or another.... Exactly what happens is that one touches these things, has experiences, and then it gets veiled, and one wonders, 'How is it that I touched my soul and now have fallen back into this state of ignorance and inconscience!' But that's because one had not touched one's soul, one had touched those parts of the being which are under the influence of the soul and manifest something of it, but are not it." (p. 46)

Such contacts with the psychic-mental or the psychic-vital are brief-lived periods which come and go.

As the psychic grows stronger with the practice of sadhana, contact with the psychic is more and more readily obtained.

A time comes when one can obtain the contact at will.

> "...as soon as one concentrates and aspires, one gets a contact. One may not have the power of keeping it all the time, but can get it at will. Then, from that moment things become very easy. When one feels a difficulty or there is a problem to be solved, when one wants to make progress or there is just a depression to conquer or an obstacle to be overcome or else simply for the joy of identification ... then, at any moment whatever, one may pause, concentrate for a while and aspire, and quite naturally the contact is established and all problems which were to be solved are solved. Simply to concentrate — to sit down and concentrate — to aspire in this way, and the contact is made, so to say, instantaneously." (pp. 43-44)

As a rule, it is only after a very long and intense sadhana that one obtains a total identification and permanent union with the psychic which brings a conscious and constant psychic contact that is never lost.

> "...it [contact with the psychic being] is in the depths of the consciousness and supports all that you do, and you never lose the contact. Then many things disappear. For instance, depression is one of these things, discontentment, revolt, fatigue, depression, all these difficulties. And if one makes it a habit to step back, as we say, in one's consciousness and see on the screen of one's psychic consciousness — see all the circumstances, all the events, all the ideas, all the knowledge, everything — at

that moment one sees *that* and has an altogether sure guide for everything that one may do. But this, perforce, takes a very long time to come." (p. 44)

When one has attained a complete identification and union with the psychic, one is said to have discovered one's soul. The psychic being is said to be awakened, no longer veiled by the mental, the vital and the physical. "When the psychic being awakens, you grow conscious of your own soul; you know your self. And you no longer commit the mistake of identifying yourself with the mental or with the vital being. You do not mistake them for the soul" (p. 86). A radical change of consciousness amounting to a reversal of consciousness takes place: the ordinary consciousness, in which one identifies oneself with the mental, vital and physical, is replaced by the psychic consciousness in which one is identified with one's soul.

How can one know if one is in contact with the psychic? To a child who asked how one can know whether the psychic being is in front or not, the Mother replied:

"...doesn't one feel it? It doesn't make a difference?... (*The child nods in assent.*) Ah!... There is not one of you who will dare to tell me that it makes no difference when the psychic is there, when one feels better within oneself, when one is full of light, hope, goodwill, generosity, compassion for the world, and sees life as a field of action, progress, realisation. Doesn't it make a difference from the days when one is bored, grumbling, when everything seems ugly, unpleasant, wicked, when one loves nobody, wants to break everything, gets angry, feels ill at ease, without strength, without energy, without any joy? That makes a difference, doesn't it?" (p. 91)

In another context, describing the state of those whose psychic is in the front of the consciousness, the Mother observes:

"Everything seems beautiful and good to them, their health improves, their consciousness grows more luminous; they feel happy, peaceful and safe; they think that they have reached their utmost possibility of consciousness. This peace and fullness and joy given by the psychic contact they naturally find everywhere, in everything and everybody." (pp. 51-52)

Thus one "in whom the contact has been well established is always happy" (p. 62). When the contact with the psychic amounts to even a brief identification with the psychic, it produces "an experience that gives a very concrete joy; at the moment of identification one truly feels a very, very great joy" (p. 44).

Joy is also the hallmark of the aspiration which comes from a contact with the psychic distinguishing it from aspiration which comes from other parts of the being. In answer to the question as to why an intense aspiration is sometimes mixed with anguish and sometimes containing joy, the Mother explains:

"As soon as the presence of the psychic consciousness is

united with the aspiration, the intensity takes on quite a different character, as if it were filled with the very essence of an inexpressible joy. This joy is something that seems contained in everything else. Whatever may be the outer form of the aspiration, whatever difficulties and obstacles it may meet, this joy is there as though it filled up everything, and it carries you in spite of everything.

That is the sure sign of the psychic presence. That is to say, you have established a contact with your psychic consciousness, a more or less complete, more or less constant contact, but at that moment it is the psychic being, the psychic consciousness which fills your aspiration, gives it its true contents. And that's what is translated into joy.

When that is not there, the aspiration may come from different parts of the being; it may come mainly from the mind or mainly from the vital or even from the physical, or it may come from all the three together — it may come from all kinds of combinations."[7]

When the contact becomes constant due to a definitive identification and union with the psychic being, one has "the feeling of immortality, of having always been and being always, eternally" (pp. 61-62).

With a definitive contact one has even the memory of one's past lives.

7. The Mother, *Questions and Answers 1956*, Collected Works of the Mother, Vol. 8, p. 250.

"When you enter into contact with the psychic you become conscious of all the lives you have lived, it keeps the absolutely living memory of all the events in which the psychic took part...." (p. 60)

And since the psychic is the Divine in the human being, when one is in constant contact with the psychic one feels "in contact with the divine Presence all the time, in all things". (p. 55)

On the other hand, when one is anxious or fearful, morose or depressed, excited or peevish, critical or complaining, or under the sway of any other egoistic state, one is clearly not in contact with the psychic at that moment.

Emergence of the Psychic

Contact with the psychic in the sense of a transient identification with it is not enough to make it the leader and governor of the being. The mind, the vital and body — which normally govern the human being — need to undergo a conversion so as to become the docile instruments of the psychic. The first necessity in order that the conversion may take place is the awakening of the psychic being. The psychic is said to be awakened when one becomes conscious of one's soul and knows the soul to be one's self, instead of identifying oneself with mind, vital and body. When the psychic being awakens, it begins to emerge or come forward and "to take hold of the rest of the being, to influence it and change it so that all may become the true expression of the inner soul" (p. 86). The influence of the psychic then becomes more direct and more conscious unlike the indirect and unconscious influence of the psychic in the early stages of growth. For by emergence or the coming in front of the psychic is meant that "it comes from behind the veil, its presence is felt already in the waking daily consciousness, its influence fills, dominates, transforms the mind and vital and their movements, even the physical" (p. 90).[8] As the psychic emerges more and more

"...it takes up its greater function as the guide and ruler of the nature. A guidance, a governance begins from within which exposes every movement to the light of Truth, repels what is false, obscure, opposed to the divine realisation: every region of the being, every nook and corner of it, every movement, formation, direction, inclination of thought, will, emotion, sensation, action, reaction, motive, disposition, propensity, desire, habit of the conscious or subconscious physical, even the most concealed, camouflaged, mute, recondite, is lighted up with the unerring

8. The coming in front of the psychic in the sense of its emergence should be distinguished from what the Mother has described as the psychic's being "in front" in little children. The psychic being is said to be in the front in little children in the sense that it is relatively more on the surface of the consciousness as compared to their later age when, as a result of development of the mind, the psychic being recedes behind and the mind is more in the forefront. In the state of emergence one is identified with one's psychic being and considers it as one's true being, whereas a little child, even though its psychic is relatively more in front, is identified with its vital and its body, not with its psychic being.

psychic light, their confusions dissipated, their tangles disentangled, their obscurities, deceptions, self-deceptions precisely indicated and removed; all is purified, set right, the whole nature harmonised, modulated in the psychic key, put in spiritual order." (pp. 104-105)

Thus it is by its emergence that the psychic being "begins to prepare the upbuilding of divinity in the earthly nature." (p. 19)

Transformation

"The upbuilding of divinity in the earthly nature" as a result of the action of the psychic and the higher consciousness is what is meant by transformation. In the spiritual evolution of mankind, the goal hitherto has been the attainment of liberation from the bondage and suffering imposed by mind, life and body. Such a liberation has been sought either by discovering one's soul and thereby attaining union with the Divine, or by stilling the mind and spiritualising it "in some kind of static liberation or Nirvana" (p. vii). In either case, one lets the instruments of mind, life and body continue acting according to their ignorant nature. But the inevitable evolutionary destiny of the human being, says Sri Aurobindo, is to go beyond liberation and achieve a transformation of the mental, vital and physical nature by bringing down the divine consciousness into the lower ignorant nature so as "to transform the Prakriti of Ignorance into a Prakriti of Knowledge." (p. 4)

Sri Aurobindo speaks of three transformations: psychic,

spiritual and supramental. Psychic transformation consists in "bringing right vision into the mind, right impulse and feeling into the vital, right movement and habit into the physical — all turned towards the Divine...."[9] By spiritual transformation is meant "the descent of the higher peace, force, light, knowledge, purity, Ananda, etc. which belong to any of the higher planes"[10] of mind above the ordinary mind. Supramental transformation "is a putting on of the spiritual consciousness, dynamic as well as static, in every part of the being down to the subconscient";[11] some of the ultimate results of the supramental transformation include "the release from subconscient ignorance and from disease, duration of life at will, and a change in the functionings of the body".[12]

Psychic transformation is the first necessity, "because it makes safe and easy the descent of the higher consciousness and the spiritual transformation without which the supramental must always remain far distant" (p. 100).

A. S. DALAL

9. Sri Aurobindo, *Letters on Yoga*, SABCL Vol. 23, p. 1093.
10. Sri Aurobindo, *Letters on Yoga*, SABCL Vol. 22, p. 106.
11. *Ibid.,* p. 116.
12. *Ibid.,* p. 8.

THE PSYCHIC BEING — ITS NATURE AND FUNCTION

The psychic has two aspects — there is the soul principle itself which contains all soul possibilities and there is the psychic personality which represents whatever soul-power is developed from life to life or put forward for action in our present life-formation. The psychic being usually expresses itself through its instruments, mental, vital and physical; it tries to put as much of its own stamp on them as possible. But it can seldom put on them the full psychic stamp — unless it comes fully out from its rather secluded and overshadowed position and takes into its hands the direct government of the nature. It can then receive and express all spiritual realisations in its own way and manner.[1]   — SRI AUROBINDO

*

At the beginning the soul in Nature, the psychic entity, whose unfolding is the first step towards a spiritual change, is an entirely veiled part of us, although it is that by which we exist and persist as individual beings in Nature. The other parts of our natural composition are not only mutable but perishable; but the psychic entity in us persists and is fundamentally the same always: it contains all essential possibilities of our manifestation but is not constituted by them; it is not limited by what it manifests, not contained by the incomplete forms of the manifestation, not tarnished by the imperfections and impurities, the defects and depravations of the surface being. It is an ever-pure flame of the divinity in things and nothing that comes to it, nothing that enters into our experience can pollute its purity or extinguish the flame. This spiritual stuff is immaculate and luminous and, because it is perfectly luminous, it is immediately, intimately, directly aware of truth of being and truth of nature; it is deeply conscious of truth and good and beauty because truth and good and beauty are akin to its own native character, forms of something that is inherent in its own substance. It is aware also of all that contradicts these things, of all that deviates from its own native character, of falsehood and evil and the ugly and the unseemly; but it does not become these things nor is it touched or changed by these opposites of itself which so powerfully affect its outer instrumentation of mind, life and body. For the soul, the permanent being in us, puts forth and uses mind, life and body as its instruments, undergoes the envelopment of their conditions, but it is other and greater than its members.

If the psychic entity had been from the beginning unveiled and known to its ministers, not a secluded King in a screened chamber, the human evolution would have been a rapid soul-outflowering, not the difficult, chequered and disfigured development it now is; but the veil is thick and we know not the secret Light within us, the light in the hidden crypt of the heart's innermost sanctuary. Intimations rise to our surface from the psyche, but our mind does not detect their source; it takes them for its own activities because, before even they come to the surface, they are clothed in mental substance:

thus ignorant of their authority, it follows or does not follow them according to its bent or turn at the moment. If the mind obeys the urge of the vital ego, then there is little chance of the psyche at all controlling the nature or manifesting in us something of its secret spiritual stuff and native movement; or, if the mind is over-confident to act in its own smaller light, attached to its own judgment, will and action of knowledge, then also the soul will remain veiled and quiescent and wait for the mind's farther evolution. For the psychic part within is there to support the natural evolution, and the first natural evolution must be the development of body, life and mind, successively, and these must act each in its own kind or together in their ill-assorted partnership in order to grow and have experience and evolve. The soul gathers the essence of all our mental, vital and bodily experience and assimilates it for the farther evolution of our existence in Nature; but this action is occult and not obtruded on the surface. In the early material and vital stages of the evolution of being there is indeed no consciousness of soul; there are psychic activities, but the instrumentation, the form of these activities are vital and physical, — or mental when the mind is active. For even the mind, so long as it is primitive or is developed but still too external, does not recognise their deeper character. It is easy to regard ourselves as physical beings or beings of life or mental beings using life and body and to ignore the existence of the soul altogether: for the only definite idea that we have of the soul is of something that survives the death of our bodies; but what this is we do not know because even if we are conscious sometimes of its presence, we are not normally

conscious of its distinct reality nor do we feel clearly its
direct action in our nature.[2]   — SRI AUROBINDO

*

The soul or psyche is immutable only in the sense that it
contains all the possibilities of the Divine within it, but it has
to evolve them and in its evolution it assumes the form of a
developing psychic individual evolving in the manifestation
the individual Prakriti and taking part in the evolution. It is
the spark of the Divine Fire that grows behind the mind, vital
and physical by means of the psychic being until it is able to
transform the Prakriti of Ignorance into a Prakriti of Knowledge. This evolving psychic being is not therefore at any time
all that the soul or essential psychic existence bears within it;
it temporalises and individualises what is eternal in potenti-
ality, transcendent in essence, in this projection of the spirit.

The central being is the being which presides over the different births one after the other, but is itself unborn, for it
does not descend into the being but is above it — it holds
together the mental, vital and physical being and all the various parts of the personality and it controls the life either
through the mental being and the mental thought and will or
through the psychic, whichever may happen to be most in
front or most powerful in nature. If it does not exercise its
control, then the consciousness is in great disorder and every
part of the personality acts for itself so that there is no coher-
ence in the thought, feeling or action.

The psychic is not above but behind — its seat is behind
the heart, its power is not knowledge but an essential or

spiritual feeling — it has the clearest sense of the Truth and a sort of inherent perception of it which is of the nature of soul-perception and soul-feeling. It is our inmost being and supports all the others, mental, vital, physical, but it is also much veiled by them and has to act upon them as an influence rather than by its sovereign right of direct action; its direct action becomes normal and preponderant only at a high stage of development or by yoga. It is not the psychic being which, you feel, gives you the intuitions of things to be or warns you against the results of certain actions; that is some part of the inner being, sometimes the inner mental, sometimes the inner vital, sometimes, it may be, the inner or subtle physical Purusha. The inner being — inner mind, inner vital, inner or subtle physical — knows much that is unknown to the outer mind, the outer vital, the outer physical, for it is in a more direct contact with the secret forces of Nature. The psychic is the inmost being of all; a perception of truth which is inherent in the deepest substance of the consciousness, a sense of the good, true, beautiful, the Divine, is its privilege.[3]

Sri Aurobindo

*

The soul is the witness, upholder, experiencer, but it is master only in theory, in fact it is not-master, *anīśa*, so long as it consents to the Ignorance. For that is a general consent which implies that the Prakriti gambols about with the Purusha and does pretty well what she likes with him. When he wants to get back his mastery, make the theoretical practical, he needs a lot of tapasya to do it. The psychic has always been veiled, consenting to the play of mind, physical and vital, experiencing everything through them in the ignorant mental, vital and physical way. How then can it be that they are bound to change at once when it just takes the trouble to whisper or say, "Let there be Light"? They have a tremendous negating power and can refuse and do refuse point-blank. The mind resists with an obstinate persistency in argument and a constant confusion of ideas, the vital with a fury of bad will aided by the mind's obliging reasonings on its side, the physical resists with an obstinate inertia and crass fidelity to old habit, and when they have done, the general Nature comes in and says, "What, you are going to get free from me so easily? Not, if I know it," and it besieges and throws back the old nature on you again and again as long as it can.[4]

SRI AUROBINDO

*

At a certain stage in the Yoga when the mind is sufficiently quieted and no longer supports itself at every step on the sufficiency of its mental certitudes, when the vital has been steadied and subdued and is no longer constantly insistent on its own rash will, demand and desire, when the physical has been sufficiently altered not to bury altogether the inner flame under the mass of its outwardness, obscurity or inertia, an inmost being, long hidden within and felt only in its rare influences, is able to come forward and illumine the rest and take up the lead of the Sadhana. Its character is a one-pointed orientation towards the Divine or the Highest, one-pointed and yet plastic in action and movement; it does not create a rigidity of direction like the one-pointed intellect or a bigotry of the regnant idea or impulse like the one-pointed vital force; it is at every moment and with a supple sureness that it points the way to the Truth, automatically distinguishes the right step from the false, extricates the divine or Godward movement from the clinging mixture of the undivine. Its action is like a searchlight showing up all that has to be changed in the nature; it has in it a flame of will insistent on perfection, on an alchemic transmutation of all the inner and outer existence. It sees the divine essence everywhere but rejects the mere mask and the disguising figure. It insists on Truth, on will and strength and mastery, on Joy and Love and Beauty, but on a Truth of abiding Knowledge that surpasses the mere practical momentary truth of the Ignorance, on an inward joy and not on mere vital pleasure, — for it prefers rather a purifying suffering and sorrow to degrading satisfactions, — on love winged upward and not tied to the stake of egoistic craving or with its feet sunk in the mire, on beauty restored to its priesthood of interpretation of the Eternal, on strength and will and mastery as instruments not of the ego but of the Spirit. Its will is for the divinisation of life, the expression through it of a higher Truth, its dedication to the Divine and the Eternal.

But the most intimate character of the psychic is its pressure towards the Divine through a sacred love, joy and oneness. It is a divine Love that it seeks most, it is the love of the Divine that is its spur, its goal, its star of Truth shining over the luminous cave of the nascent or the still obscure cradle of the new-born godhead within us. In the first long stage of its growth and immature existence it has leaned on earthly love, affection, tenderness, goodwill, compassion, benevolence, on all beauty and gentleness and fineness and light and strength and courage, on all that can help to refine and purify the grossness and commonness of human nature; but it knows how mixed are these human movements at their best and at their worst how fallen and stamped with the mark of ego and self-deceptive sentimental falsehood and the lower self profiting by the imitation of a soul-movement. At once, emerging, it is ready and eager to break all the old ties and imperfect emotional activities and replace them by a greater spiritual Truth of love and oneness. It may still admit the human forms and movements, but on condition that they are turned towards the One alone. It accepts only the ties that are helpful, the heart's and mind's reverence for the Guru, the union of the God-seekers, a spiritual compassion for this ignorant human and animal world and its peoples, the joy and happiness and satisfaction of beauty that comes from the perception of the Divine everywhere. It plunges the nature inward towards its meeting with the immanent Divine in the heart's secret centre and, while that call is there, no reproach of egoism, no mere outward summons of altruism or duty or philanthropy or service will deceive or divert it from its sacred longing and its obedience to the attraction of the Divinity within it. It lifts the being towards a transcendent Ecstasy and is ready to shed all the downward pull of the world from its wings in its uprising to reach the One Highest; but it calls down also this transcendent Love and Beatitude to deliver and transform this world of hatred and strife and division and darkness and jarring Ignorance. It opens to a universal Divine Love, a vast compassion, an intense and immense will for the good of all, for the embrace of the World-Mother enveloping or gathering to her her children, the divine Passion that has plunged into the night for the redemption of the world from the universal Inconscience. It is not attracted or misled by mental imitations or any vital misuse of these great deep-seated Truths of existence; it exposes them with its detecting search-ray and calls down the entire truth of divine Love to heal these malformations, to deliver mental, vital, physical love from their insufficiencies or their perversions and reveal to them their true abounding share of the intimacy and the oneness, the ascending ecstasy and the descending rapture.[5]

Sri Aurobindo

*

I did not understand the explanation of the psychic you have given:

"One could say, for example, that the creation of an individual being is the result of the projection, in time and space, of one of the countless possibilities latent in the supreme origin of all manifestation which, through the medium of the one and universal consciousness, takes concrete form in the law or the truth of an individual and so, by a progressive development, becomes his soul or psychic being." — The Mother

It is a little philosophical…. You know the difference between what is subjective and what is objective? You know it! Well, imagine precisely this Reality we were speaking about, which is at the origin of all things, passing from the subjective to the objective state. That is, what was within becomes as though projected outside. It is the *same* thing: it is the state that changes. And so, within it there are all the possibilities of objective existence; within they are unexpressed, unmanifested; outside they are projected, as a picture is projected on the cinema-screen: we see it before us. And every element that was a possibility within, a law, becomes the law of a realisation. And every one of these possibilities becomes the reality of a being, of an individuality if you like, of something existing objectively. And it is that law which is the origin of the centre of the psychic being: it is the truth of the being or the law of the being. The Buddha called it the "law", he spoke of the *Dharma*. It is the truth of the being. It is that which binds it again indestructibly to its origin. And that is the starting-point of the psychic being. And so, even as this develops, like the picture on the screen, it takes a more and more complex and precise form in the manifestation. But the reality of that form is one, it is bound to the One. And all the units are linked together and reproduce the One.[6]

THE MOTHER

*

The true self and the psychic are the same thing?

No. The true self is what is also called the truth of the being. It is the divine element which is your individual reality. It is the divine element which makes you a separate individuality, and it is at the same time a fragment of the one Being and naturally the one Being itself; that is, while being a particular aspect which makes you an individual, it is an integral part of the One which makes you only an objectivisation of the One.

This is the true self. The psychic being is a terrestrial formation. It is human beings who have a psychic being which has been developed upon earth and by earthly life and which is a projection of the divine Consciousness into Matter to awaken Matter out of its inertia so that it takes the path back to the Divine.

But in certain cases the true self is found in the psychic being, that is, it dwells in the psychic being — but not always.

There is always a divine Presence in the psychic being, but it is the divine Presence which was at the origin of the psychic formation, it is an emanation from the divine Consciousness; whereas the true self is not a terrestrial formation. It precedes the terrestrial formation.[7]   — THE MOTHER

⁂

The psychic being is formed by the inner Truth and organised around it.[8]   — THE MOTHER

*

Does the psychic being identify itself with the inner Truth?

It organises itself around it and enters into contact with it. The psychic is moved by the Truth. The Truth is something eternally self-existent and dependent on nothing in time or space, whereas the psychic being is a being that grows, takes form, progresses, individualises itself more and more. In this way it becomes more and more capable of manifesting this Truth, the eternal Truth that is one and permanent. The psychic being is a progressive being, which means that the relation between the psychic being and the Truth is a progressive one. It is not possible to become aware of one's psychic being without becoming aware at the same time of the inner Truth. All those who have had this experience — not a mental experience but an integral experience of contact with the psychic being, not a contact with the idea they have constructed of it, but a truly concrete contact — all say the same thing: from the very minute this contact takes place, one is absolutely conscious of the eternal Truth within oneself and one sees that it is the purpose of life and the guide of the world. One can't have one without the other; in fact, it is this that makes you realise that you are in contact with your psychic being. It may not be a conscious contact, but something that governs your life.

Some people say there is something outside their own will that organises their whole life, that puts them in the required condition, that attracts favourable circumstances or people, that arranges everything outside them, so to say. In their outer consciousness, perhaps they wanted something and worked for it, but something else came. Well, after some years, they realise that this is what really had to happen. You may know nothing of the existence of a psychic being within you and yet be guided by it. For, in order to become aware of something, you must first of all admit that this thing exists. Some people don't. I have known people who had a genuine contact with their psychic being without knowing at all what it was, because there was nothing in them that corresponded to the knowledge of this contact.[9]   — THE MOTHER

*

The other day I said that most of the time people do not have their psychic being within them. I would like to explain this in greater detail.... You must remember that the inner beings are not in the third dimension. If you open up your body you will find only the viscera of the body which are in the third dimension. The inner beings are in another dimension, and when I say that some men do not have their psychic being within them, I do not mean that it is not at the centre of their being, but that their outer consciousness is so small, so limited, so obscure that it is not able to keep a contact, not only conscious but intimate, with the psychic being which extends beyond it in every way; it is so much higher and deeper than the other outer consciousness that there is no relation either of quality or of nature between them. Religions say that you have a divine spark in you — it is well they call it a "spark", for it is so small indeed that it can be placed anywhere in the body without difficulty. But this does not mean that it is in the body: it is within the consciousness in another dimension, and there are beings who have a contact with it, others who haven't. But if you come to the divine Presence in the atom, the image is easier to understand, for there you touch so infinitesimal a domain that you are on the borderline where you can no longer distinguish between two, three, four or five dimensions. If you study modern physics you will understand what I mean. The movements

constituting an atom are, in the matter of size, so impercepti-
ble that they cannot be understood with our three-dimensional
understanding, the more so as they follow laws which elude
completely this three-dimensional idea. So if you take refuge
there, you may say that the divine spark is at the centre of each
atom and you won't be far from the truth; but I was not speaking of the divine spark, I was speaking of the being, the psychic consciousness, which is another thing. The psychic being
is an entity which has a form; it is organised around a central
consciousness and, having a form it has a dimension, but a
dimension of another kind than the third dimension of the outer
consciousness.[10]   — THE MOTHER

*

The psychic being is the representative of the Divine in the
human being. That's it, you see — the Divine is not something remote and inaccessible. The Divine is in you but you
are not fully conscious of it. Rather you have... it acts now
as an influence rather than as a Presence. It should be a conscious Presence, you should be able at each moment to ask
yourself what is... how the Divine sees. It is like that: first
how the Divine sees, and then how the Divine wills, and then
how the Divine acts. And it is not to go away into inaccessible regions, it is right here. Only, for the moment, all the old
habits and the general unconsciousness put a kind of cover-
ing which prevents us from seeing and feeling. You must...
you must lift, you must lift that up.[11]   — THE MOTHER

*

The psychic world or plane of consciousness is that part of the world, the psychic being is that part of the being which is directly under the influence of the Divine Consciousness.... It is a world of harmony, and everything moves in it from light to light and from progress to progress. It is the seat of the Divine Consciousness, the Divine Self in the individual being. It is a centre of light and truth and knowledge and beauty and harmony which the Divine Self in each of you creates by his presence, little by little; it is influenced, formed and moved by the Divine Consciousness of which it is a part and parcel. It is in each of you the deep inner being which you have to find in order that you may come in contact with the Divine in you. It is the intermediary between the Divine Consciousness and your external consciousness; it is the builder of the inner life, it is that which manifests in the outer nature the order and rule of the Divine Will. If you become aware in your outer consciousness of the psychic being within you and unite with it, you can find the pure Eternal Consciousness and live in it; instead of being moved by the Ignorance as the human being constantly is, you grow aware of the presence of an eternal light and knowledge within you, and to it you surrender and are integrally consecrated to it and moved by it in all things.

For your psychic being is that part of you which is already given to the Divine. It is its influence gradually spreading from within towards the most outward and material boundaries of your consciousness that will bring about the transformation of your entire nature. There can be no obscurity here; it is the luminous part in you. Most people are unconscious of this psychic part within them; the effort of Yoga is to make you conscious of it, so that the process of your transformation, instead of a slow labour extending through centuries, can be pressed into one life or even a few years.

The psychic being is that which persists after death, because it is your eternal self; it is this that carries the consciousness forward from life to life.

The psychic being is the real individuality of the true and divine individual within you. For your individuality means your special mode of expression and your psychic being is a special aspect of the one Divine Consciousness that has taken shape in you. But in the psychic consciousness there is not that sense of division between the individual and the universal consciousness which affects the other parts of your nature. You are conscious there that your individuality is your own line of expression, but at the same time you know too that it is an expression objectifying the one universal consciousness. It is as though you had taken a portion out of yourself and put it in front of you and there were a mutual look and play of movement between the two. This duality was necessary in order to create and establish the objectivised relation and to enjoy it; but in your psychic being the separation that sharpens the duality is seen to be an illusion, an appearance and nothing more.[12]   — THE MOTHER

*

You must learn to unite what you call your individual self with your true psychic individuality. Your present individuality is a very mixed thing, a series of changes which yet preserves a certain continuity, a certain sameness or identity of vibration in the midst of all flux. It is almost like a river which is never the same and yet has a certain definiteness and persistence of its own. Your normal self is merely a shadow of your true individuality which you will realise only when this normal individual which is differently poised at different times, now in the mental, then in the vital, at other times in the physical, gets into contact with the psychic and feels it as its real being. Then you will be one, nothing will shake or disturb you, you will make steady and lasting progress....[13]

THE MOTHER

*

The psychic being is in the heart centre in the middle of the chest (not in the physical heart, for all the centres are in the middle of the body), but it is deep behind. When one is going away from the vital into the psychic, it is felt as if one is going deep deep down till one reaches that central place of the psychic. The surface of the heart centre is the place of the emotional being; from there one goes deep to find the psychic. The more one goes, the more intense becomes the psychic happiness....[14]   — SRI AUROBINDO

*

Man, because he is a mental being, is prone to give the highest importance to the thinking mind and its reason and will and to its way of approach and effectuation of Truth and, even, he is inclined to hold that there is no other. The heart with its emotions and incalculable movements is to the eye of his intellect an obscure, uncertain and often a perilous and misleading power which needs to be kept in control by the reason and the mental will and intelligence. And yet there is in the heart or behind it a profounder mystic light which, if not what we call intuition, — for that, though not of the mind, yet descends through the mind, — has yet a direct touch upon Truth and is nearer to the Divine than the human intellect in its pride of knowledge. According to the ancient teaching the seat of the immanent Divine, the hidden Purusha, is in the mystic heart, — the secret heart-cave, *hṛdaye guhāyām*, as the Upanishads put it, — and, according to the experience of many Yogins, it is from its depths that there comes the voice or the breath of the inner oracle.

This ambiguity, these opposing appearances of depth and blindness are created by the double character of the human emotive being. For there is in front in man a heart of vital emotion similar to the animal's, if more variously developed; its emotions are governed by egoistic passion, blind instinctive affections and all the play of the life-impulses with their imperfections, perversions, often sordid degradations, — a heart besieged and given over to the lusts, desires, wraths, intense or fierce demands or little greeds and mean pettinesses of an obscure and fallen life-force and debased by its slavery to any and every impulse. This mixture of the emotive heart and the sensational hungering vital creates in man a false soul of desire; it is this that is the crude and dangerous element which the reason rightly distrusts and feels a need to control, even though the actual control or rather coercion it succeeds in establishing over our raw and insistent vital nature remains always very uncertain and deceptive. But the true soul of man is not there; it is in the true invisible heart hidden in some luminous cave of the nature: there under some infiltration of the divine Light is our soul, a silent inmost being of which few are even aware; for if all have a soul, few are conscious of their true soul or feel its direct impulse. There dwells the little spark of the Divine which supports the obscure mass of our nature and around it grows the psychic being, the formed soul or the real Man within us. It is as this psychic being in him grows and the movements of the heart reflect its divinations and impulsions that man becomes more and more aware of his soul, ceases to be a superior animal and, awakening to glimpses of the godhead within him, admits more and more its intimations of a deeper life and consciousness and an impulse towards things divine. It is one of the decisive moments of the integral Yoga when this psychic being, liberated, brought out from the veil to the front, can pour the full flood of its divinations, seeings and impulsions on the mind, life and body of man and begins to prepare the upbuilding of divinity in the earthly nature.[15]

SRI AUROBINDO

*

... you must not mistake the feelings for the psychic, you understand! — these two are absolutely different things. People always think that when they have emotions, feelings, they are entering the psychic. These things have nothing to do with the psychic, they are purely vital. They are the most subtle part of the vital, if you like, but they are vital. It's not through the feelings that one goes to the psychic, it is through a very intense aspiration and a self-detachment.[16]

THE MOTHER

*

Don't mix up the psychic being with the outer being. The psychic being may be perfect and the outer being may be idiotic. Don't confuse the two. They have nothing to do... unfortunately they have nothing to do with each other, most of the time. For the outer being is not at all conscious of the psychic being; but to the extent that it is conscious it reflects the perfection of this psychic.[17]   — THE MOTHER

*

There is the true psychic which is always good and there is the psychic opening to mental, vital and other worlds which contain all kinds of things good, bad and indifferent, true, false and half true, thought-suggestions which are of all kinds, and messages also which are of all kinds. What is needed is not to give yourself impartially to all of them but to develop both a sufficient knowledge and experience and a sufficient discrimination to be able to keep your balance and eliminate falsehood, half-truths and mixtures.[18]   — SRI AUROBINDO

*

The fundamental seat of aspiration from which it [aspiration] radiates or manifests in one part of the being or another is the psychic centre.[19]   — THE MOTHER

*

All urge for perfection comes from it, but you are unaware of the source, you are not collaborating with it knowingly, you are not in identification with its light. Do not think I refer to the emotional part of you when I speak of the psychic. Emotion belongs to the higher vital, not to the pure psychic. The psychic is a steady flame that burns in you, soaring towards the Divine and carrying with it a sense of strength which breaks down all oppositions. When you are identified with it you have the feeling of the divine truth — then you cannot help feeling also that the whole world is ignorantly walking on its head with its feet in the air![20]   — THE MOTHER

*

Wherever…there is a spontaneous admiration for the true, the beautiful, the noble, there is something divine expressed. You should know for certain that it is the psychic being, the soul in you with which your physical consciousness comes in contact when your heart leaps out to worship and admire what you feel to be of a divine origin.[21]   — THE MOTHER

*

Indeed, the expression of a true psychic life in the being is peace, a joyful serenity.[22]   — THE MOTHER

*

In everybody, is the psychic always pure or has it to be made pure?

It is always pure. But it is either more or less individualised and independent in its action. What is psychic in the being is always pure, by its very definition, for it is that part of the being which is in contact with the Divine and expresses the truth of the being. But this may be like a spark in the darkness of the being or it may be a being of light, conscious, fully formed and independent. There are all the gradations between the two.[23]   — THE MOTHER

*

What is the difference between "spiritual" and "psychic"?

It is not the same thing. The psychic is the being organised by the divine Presence and it belongs to the earth — I am not speaking of the universe, only of the earth; it is only upon earth that you will find the psychic being. The rest of the universe is formed in quite a different way.

The universe contains all the domains higher than the physical: there is a global physical comprising the mental, the vital, etc., and all the domains above the mental are domains of a spiritual order, domains which are, for us, domains of the spirit, and it is this "spirit" which little by little, progressively, materialises itself to arrive at Matter as we conceive it. The beings of the Overmind, for instance, and all the beings of the higher regions have no psychic being — the "angels" have no psychic being. It is only upon earth that the psychic life begins, and it is just the process by which the Divine has awakened material life to the necessity of rejoining its divine origin. Without the psychic, Matter would never have awakened from its inconscience, it would never have aspired for the life of its origin, the spiritual life. Therefore, the psychic being in the human being is the manifestation of spiritual aspiration; but there is a spiritual life independent of the psychic.[24]   — THE MOTHER

*

Is there a difference between the "spiritual" and the "psychic"? Are they different planes?

Yes, the psychic plane belongs to the personal manifestation; the psychic is that which is divine in you put out to be dynamic in the play. But when we speak of the spiritual we are thinking of something that is concentrated in the Divine rather than in the external manifestation. The spiritual plane is something static behind and above the outward play; it supports the instruments of the nature, but is not itself included or involved in the external manifestation here.

But in speaking of these things one must be careful not to be imprisoned by the words we use. When I speak of the psychic or the spiritual, I mean things that are very deep and real behind the flat surface of the words and intimately connected even in their difference.[25]   — THE MOTHER

*

*What is the difference between the psychic change and
the spiritual change?*

The psychic change is the change that puts you in contact
with the immanent Divine, the Divine who is at the centre of
each being and of whom the psychic being is the sheath and
the expression. By the psychic change one passes from the
individual Divine to the universal Divine and finally to the
Transcendent.

The spiritual change puts you directly in contact with the
Supreme.[26]   — THE MOTHER

*

Do not confuse the psychic realisation with the spiritual realisation, because the psychic realisation will leave you within
time and space, within the manifested universe.

Whereas the effect of the spiritual realisation will be to
project you outside all creation, outside time and space.[27]

THE MOTHER

*

What is the work of the psychic being?

… What do you want to say exactly? What is its function?
Ah! Very well. One could put it this way, that it is like an
electric wire that connects the generator with the lamp. Now,
if someone has understood, let him explain what I said!

What is the generator and what the lamp? (Laughter)

Ah, there we are! So, what is the generator and what the lamp? That is exactly it. What is the generator and what the lamp? Or rather, who is the generator and who is the lamp?

The generator is the Divine and the lamp is the body.

It is the body, it is the visible being.

So, that is its function. This means that if there were no psychic in Matter, it would not be able to have any direct contact with the Divine. And it is happily due to this psychic presence in Matter that the contact between Matter and the Divine can be direct and all human beings can be told, "You carry the Divine within you, and you have only to enter within yourself and you will find Him." It is something very particular to the human being or rather to the inhabitants of the earth. In the human being the psychic becomes more conscious, more formed, more conscious and more independent also. It is individualised in human beings. But it is a speciality of the earth. It is a direct infusion, special and redeeming, in the most inconscient and obscure Matter, so that it might once again awake through stages to the divine Consciousness, the divine Presence and finally to the Divine Himself. It is the presence of the psychic which makes man an exceptional being — I don't like to tell him this very much, because already he thinks too much of himself; he has such a high opinion of himself that it is not necessary to encourage him! But still, this is a fact — so much so that there are beings of other domains of the universe, those called by some people demigods and even gods, beings, for instance, of what Sri Aurobindo calls the Overmind, who are very eager to take a physical body on earth to have the experience of the psychic, for they don't have it. These beings certainly have many qualities that men don't, but they lack this divine presence which is altogether exceptional and exists only on the earth and nowhere else. All these inhabitants of the higher worlds, the Higher Mind, Overmind and other regions have no psychic being. Of course, the beings of the vital worlds don't have it either. But these latter don't regret it, they don't want it. There are only those very rare ones, quite exceptional, who want to be converted, and for this they act without delay, they immediately take a physical body. The others don't want it; it is something which binds them and constrains them to a rule they do not want.

But it is a fact, so I am obliged to state that this is how it is, that it is an exceptional quality of the human being to carry within himself the psychic and, truly speaking, he does not take full advantage from it. He does not seem to consider this quality as something very, very desirable, from the way he treats this presence — exactly that! He prefers to it the ideas of his mind, prefers the desires of his vital being and the habits of his physical.

I don't know how many of you have read the Bible; it is not very entertaining to read it, and besides, it is very long, but still, in the Bible there is a story I have always liked very much. There were two brothers, if I am not mistaken, Esau and Jacob. Well, Esau was very hungry, that's the story, isn't it? I believe he was a hunter or something; anyway, the story goes like this. He came back home very hungry, and told

Jacob he was very hungry, and he was so hungry that he said to him, "Listen, if you give me your mess of pottage" (Jacob had prepared some stew), "if you give me your mess of pottage I will give you my birthright." You know, one can understand the story quite superficially, but it has a very profound meaning: the birthright is the right of being the son of God. And so he was quite ready to give up his divine right because he was hungry, for a concrete, material thing, for food. This is a very old story, but it is eternally true.[28]   — THE MOTHER

*

... from the very moment of birth in a physical body, there is in the being, in its depths, this psychic presence which pushes the whole being towards this fulfilment [discovery of one's divine Self]. But who knows it and recognises it, this psychic being? That too comes only in special circumstances, and unfortunately, most of the time these have to be painful circumstances, otherwise one goes on living unthinkingly. And in the depths of one's being is this psychic being which seeks, seeks, seeks to awaken the consciousness and re-establish the union [with one's divine Self]. One knows nothing about it.[29]

THE MOTHER

*

> *Mother, does an individual's life depend on the experience his psychic being wants to have?*

Very much!

I was speaking about just this with someone today, and I said this, that if one can become fully conscious of his psychic being, at the same time one understands, necessarily, the reason of his present existence and the experience this psychic being wants to have; and instead of having it somewhat half consciously and more than half unconsciously, one can shorten this experience and so help his psychic being to cover in a limited number of years the experiences it would perhaps take several lifetimes to go through. That is to say, the help is reciprocal. The psychic, when it has an influence on the outer life, brings to it light, order and quietude and the joy of the divine contact. But also the physical being, the body-consciousness, if it is identified with the psychic consciousness, and through that learns what kind of experience the psychic being wants to have, it can help it to have these experiences in a very brief time, and not only save time but save many lives for the psychic being. It is a mutual help.

In brief, this is what yoga means. Yoga helps you to become fully conscious of your destiny, that is, your mission in the universe, and not only at the present moment but what it was in the past and what it will be in the future. And because of this knowledge you can gather by a concentration of the consciousness all these experiences in a very short time and gain lives, do in a few years what could take a fairly considerable number of lives to achieve. The psychic being goes progressively through all these experiences towards its full maturity and complete independence, its liberation — in the sense that it no longer needs any new life. If it wants to come back to the physical world, it returns, because it has something to do there and it chooses freely to return. But till then, till this liberation, it is compelled to return to have all the experiences it needs. Well, if it happens that once the physical being is developed and conscious enough and has enough goodwill to be able to become fully aware of the psychic being, it can then and there create all the circumstances, the outer experiences necessary for the psychic being to attain its maturity in this very life.[30]   — THE MOTHER

*

... every psychic being which is in a body has states of being formed in the present formation. Its work is always to transform these; it is as though this were the part of the universe given to him for his work of transformation. And even if he has a vaster mission than that of his own person, unless he does this work in his person he cannot do the other... You cannot change the outer world unless you begin by changing yourself. This is the first condition; and for everyone, great and small, old and young — old, I mean those who have lived very long, and young those who haven't lived very long — it is always the same work. This is why life upon earth for a psychic being is the opportunity to progress.[31]

THE MOTHER

ACTION AND INFLUENCE OF
THE PSYCHIC BEING

As the evolution proceeds, Nature begins slowly and tentatively to manifest our occult parts; she leads us to look more and more within ourselves or sets out to initiate more clearly recognisable intimations and formations of them on the surface. The soul in us, the psychic principle, has already begun to take secret form; it puts forward and develops a soul-personality, a distinct psychic being to represent it. This psychic being remains still behind the veil in our subliminal part, like the true mental, the true vital or the true or subtle physical being within us: but, like them, it acts on the surface life by the influences and intimations it throws up upon that surface; these form part of the surface aggregate which is the conglomerate effect of the inner influences and upsurgings, the visible formation and superstructure which we ordinarily experience and think of as ourselves. On this ignorant surface we become dimly aware of something that can be called a soul as distinct from mind, life or body; we feel it not only as our mental idea or vague instinct of ourselves, but as a sensible influence in our life and character and action. A certain sensitive feeling for all that is true and good and beautiful, fine and pure and noble, a response to it, a demand for it, a pressure on mind and life to accept and formulate it in our thought, feelings, conduct, character is the most usually recognised, the most general and characteristic, though not the sole sign of this influence of the

psyche. Of the man who has not this element in him or does
not respond at all to this urge, we say that he has no soul.
For it is this influence that we can most easily recognise as a
finer or even a diviner part in us and the most powerful for
the slow turning towards some aim at perfection in our nature.

But this psychic influence or action does not come up to
the surface quite pure or does not remain distinct in its purity; if it did, we would be able to distinguish clearly the soul
element in us and follow consciously and fully its dictates.
An occult mental and vital and subtle-physical action inter-
venes, mixes with it, tries to use it and turn it to its own profit,
dwarfs its divinity, distorts or diminishes its self-expression,
even causes it to deviate and stumble or stains it with the
impurity, smallness and error of mind and life and body. After it reaches the surface, thus alloyed and diminished, it is
taken hold of by the surface nature in an obscure reception
and ignorant formation, and there is or can be by this cause a
still further deviation and mixture. A twist is given, a wrong
direction is imparted, a wrong application, a wrong formation, an erroneous result of what is in itself pure stuff and
action of our spiritual being; a formation of consciousness is
accordingly made which is a mixture of the psychic influence and its intimations jumbled with mental ideas and opinions, vital desires and urges, habitual physical tendencies.
There coalesce too with the obscured soul-influence the ignorant though well-intentioned efforts of these external parts
towards a higher direction; a mental ideation of a very mixed
character, often obscure even in its idealism, sometimes even
disastrously mistaken, a fervour and passion of the emotional

being throwing up its spray and foam of feelings, sentiments, sentimentalisms, a dynamic enthusiasm of the life-parts, eager responses of the physical, the thrills and excitements of nerve and body, — all these influences coalesce in a composite formation which is frequently taken as the soul and its mixed and confused action for the soul-stir, for a psychic development and action or a realised inner influence. The psychic entity is itself free from stain or mixture, but what comes up from it is not protected by that immunity; therefore this confusion becomes possible.[32]   — SRI AUROBINDO

*

For instance, take a movement, an inspiration coming from the psychic depths of the being — for it comes even to those who are not conscious of their psychic — a kind of inspiration coming from the depths; well, in order to make itself perceptible it has to come to the surface. And as it comes to the surface, it gets mixed with all sorts of things which have nothing to do with it but which want to make use of it. As, for instance, all the desires and passions of the vital which, as soon as a force from the depths rises to the surface, catch hold of it for their own satisfaction. Or else people who live in the mind and want to understand and evaluate their experience, to judge it: then it is the mind that seizes upon this inspiration or this force which rises to the surface, for its own benefit, for its own satisfaction — and it becomes mixed, and that spoils everything. And this happens constantly; constantly surface movements creep into the inspiration from the depths and deform it, veil it, defile it, ruin it completely, deforming it to such an extent that it is no longer recognisable.

> *Why do these external impulses, when they come in*
> *contact with the inspiration rising from within, spoil*
> *everything, instead of being transformed?*

Ah! excuse me, it is a reciprocal movement. And it depends on the proportion. The inspiration from within acts, of course. It is not that it is completely absorbed and destroyed, it isn't that. Necessarily, it acts but it becomes mixed, it loses its purity and original power. But all the same something remains, and the result depends on the proportion of the forces, and this proportion is very different depending on the individual.

There comes a time when one deliberately calls the deep inner inspiration and surrenders to it, when it can enter almost completely pure and make you act in accordance with the Divine Will.

The mixture is not unavoidable; it is only what usually happens. And the proportion is very different according to the individual. With some, when the psychic within takes a decision and sends out a force, it is quite visible, it is visibly a psychic inspiration. One can at times see a sort of shadow pass which comes from the mind or the vital; but these are interventions of no importance which cannot at all change the nature of the psychic inspiration, if one does not let them have the upper hand.

None of these things is irremediable, for otherwise there would be no hope of progress.[33]   — THE MOTHER

*

*What is the most effective means of awakening the
psychic being?*

But it is wide awake! And not only is it awake, but it acts,
only you are not aware of it. It appears to you asleep because you don't perceive it!

Fundamentally, without this kind of inner will of the psychic being, I believe human beings would be quite dismal,
dull, they would have an altogether animal life. Every gleam
of aspiration is always the expression of a psychic influence.
Without the presence of the psychic, without the psychic influence, there would never be any sense of progress or any
will for progress.[34]   — THE MOTHER

*

In ordinary life also there is no doubt an action of the
psychic — without it man would be only a thinking and
planning animal. But its action there is very much veiled,
needing always the mental or vital to express it, usually
mixed and not dominant, not unerring therefore; it does often the right thing in the wrong way, is moved by the right
feeling but errs as to the application, person, place, circumstances. The psychic, except in a few extraordinary natures,
does not get its full chance in the outer consciousness; it
needs some kind of Yoga or Sadhana to come by its own and
it is as it emerges more and more in front that it gets clear of
the mixture. That is to say, its presence becomes directly
felt, not only behind and supporting, but filling the frontal
consciousness and no longer dependent or dominated by its

instruments — mind, vital and body, but dominating them and moulding them into luminosity and teaching them their true action.[35]   — SRI AUROBINDO

*

It is the action of the psychic being, not the being itself, that gets mixed with the mental, vital and physical disabilities because it has to use them to express what little of the true psychic feeling gets through the veil. It is by the heart's aspiration to the Divine that the psychic gets free from these disabilities.[36]   — SRI AUROBINDO

*

The place of the psychic is deep within the heart, — but *deep within*, not on the surface where the ordinary emotions are. But it can come forward and occupy the surface as well as be within, — then the emotions themselves become no longer vital things, but psychic emotions and feelings. The psychic so standing in front can also extend its influence everywhere, to the mind for instance so as to transform its ideas or to the body so as to transform its habits and its reactions.[37]   — SRI AUROBINDO

*

You have said that once we have found our psychic being, we can never lose it. Isn't that so? But can we come into contact with it from time to time when we are receptive?

When you have established contact with your psychic being, it is, in effect, definitive.

But before this contact is established, you can, in certain
circumstances, consciously receive the psychic *influence* which
always produces an illumination in the being and has more
or less lasting effects.[38]   — THE MOTHER

*

"Our one objective must be the Divine himself to whom,
knowingly or unknowingly, something always aspires in
our secret nature."   — Sri Aurobindo, *The Synthesis of Yoga*

What is this something which aspires...?

It is a part of the being which is not always the same in everyone, and which is instinctively open to the influence of the
psychic.

There is always one part — sometimes indeed quite veiled,
of which we are not conscious — something in the being
which is turned to the psychic and receiving its influence.
This is the intermediary between the psychic consciousness
and the external consciousness.

It is not the same thing in everyone; in each one it is different. It is the point in his nature or character through which
he can touch the psychic and where he can receive the psychic influence. It depends upon people; for each one it is
different; everyone has a point like this.[39]   — THE MOTHER

*

Which part of the being aspires for love, for peace?

It is that part on any plane (physical, vital or mental) which is open to the psychic influence.[40]   — THE MOTHER

*

What does "psychic poise" mean?

Psychic poise means the poise of the being which comes from the fact that the psychic, which governs the movements of the being, is the master of all the movements of the consciousness. The psychic is always well poised. So when it is active and governs the being, it inevitably brings a balance.

... Then why is it said: "The psychic poise is necessary"?

Yes. This means that the help of the psychic poise is necessary. It is not that the psychic being has to become balanced: it is that one must be under the influence of the psychic poise. The psychic is always balanced. But the being is not always under the influence of the psychic which brings the balance. The influence of the psychic gives the balance.[41]

THE MOTHER

*

Mother, is the orientation of an individual's life directed by the psychic?

Yes. Absolutely unconsciously for the individual, most of

the time; but it is the psychic which organises his existence
— only in what may be called the main lines, because for
intervening in the details there would have to be a conscious
union between the outer being, that is, the vital and physical
being, and the psychic being, but usually this does not exist.
So externally, in the details... for example, there was someone who in deep perplexity said to me, "Well, if it is the
psychic being or rather the Divine in the psychic who directs our life, is it He who decides the number of pieces of
sugar I put in my tea-cup?" That was the question, verbatim.
So the answer had to be, "No, because it is not a detailed
intervention of this kind."

It is as when you push your fist into a heap of iron filings
or saw-dust, all the infinitesimal little elements of the iron
filings or saw-dust are organised to take on the form of your
fist, but they do not do this either deliberately or consciously.
It is through the work of the consciousness which pushes
that this kind of thing happens. There is no decision that each
element is going to be exactly in this place, like that; it is the
effect of the energy which has pushed the fist that organises
the elements. But that's how it is. There is the psychic consciousness at work in life, organising all the circumstances
of your life but not with a deliberate choice of the details....[42]

THE MOTHER

*

If you have within you a psychic being sufficiently awake to
watch over you, to prepare your path, it can draw towards
you things which help you, draw people, books, circum-

stances, all sorts of little coincidences which come to you as though brought by some benevolent will and give you an indication, a help, a support to take decisions and turn you in the right direction. But once you have taken this decision, once you have decided to find the truth of your being, once you start sincerely on the road, then everything seems to conspire to help you to advance....[43]   — THE MOTHER

*

[After death, before a new life begins, having decided to acquire a certain series of experiences in the subsequent life,] it [the psychic being] decides that at a certain moment it will take a body. Having already had a number of experiences, it knows that in a certain country, a certain part of the consciousness has developed; in another, another part, and so on; so it chooses the place which offers it easy possibilities of development: the country, the conditions of living, the approximate nature of the parents, and also the condition of the body itself, its physical structure and the qualities it needs for its experiences. It takes rest, then at the required moment, wakes up and projects its consciousness upon earth centralising it in the chosen domain and the chosen conditions — or almost so; there is a small margin you know, for in the psychic consciousness one is too far away from the material physical consciousness to be able to see with a clear vision; it is an approximation. It does not make a mistake about the country or the environment and it sees quite clearly the inner vibrations of the people chosen, but there may happen to be a slight indecision. But if, just at this moment, there is a couple upon earth or rather a woman who has a psychic aspiration herself and, for some reason or other, without knowing why or how, would like to have an exceptional child, answering certain exceptional conditions; if at this moment there is this aspiration upon earth, it creates a vibration, a psychic light which the psychic being sees immediately and, without hesitation it rushes towards it. Then, from that moment (which is the moment of conception), it watches over the formation of the child, so that this formation may be as favourable as possible to the plan it has; consequently its influence is there over the child even before it appears in the physical world.

If all goes well, if there is no accident (accidents can always happen), if all goes well at the moment the child is about to be born, the psychic force (perhaps not in its totality, but a part of the psychic consciousness) rushes into the being and from its very first cry gives it a push towards the experiences it wants the child to acquire. The result is that even if the parents are not conscious, even if the child in its external consciousness is not quite conscious (a little child does not have the necessary brain for that, it forms slowly, little by little), in spite of that, it will be possible for the psychic influence to direct all the events, all the circumstances of the life of this child till the moment it becomes capable of coming into conscious contact with its psychic being (physically it is generally between the age of four and seven, sometimes sooner, sometimes almost immediately, but in such a case we deal with children who are not "children", who have "supernatural" qualities, as they say — they are not "supernatural", but simply the expression of the presence of the psychic being). But there are people who have not had the chance or rather the good fortune if one may call it that, of meeting someone, physically, who could instruct them. And yet they have the feeling that every step of their existence, every circumstance of their life is arranged by someone conscious, so that they may make the maximum progress. When they need a certain circumstance, it comes; when they need to meet certain people, they come; when they need to read certain books, they find them within their reach. Everything is arranged like that, as if someone was watching over them so that their life may have the maximum possibilities of development. These people may very well say: "But what is a psychic being?", for no one has ever used these words in speaking to them or they have not found anybody who could explain to them all that; but for them often just one meeting is sufficient, just one look, in order to wake up, one word suffices to make them remember: "But I knew all that!"[44]

THE MOTHER

CONTACT WITH THE PSYCHIC BEING

*(All passages in this Section have been extracted
from the works of the Mother.)*

Usually is it [the psychic] veiled?

It is the outer consciousness that is not in contact with it, for
it is turned outwards instead of being turned inwards — for
it lives amidst all the external noises and movements, in what
it sees, what it does, what it says, instead of looking within,
into the depths of the being and listening to the inner inspirations.[45]

*

Sweet Mother,
    *You wrote to me that it is not easy to come in contact
with the psychic being. Why do you consider it difficult?
How should I begin?*

I said "not easy" because the contact is not spontaneous — it
is voluntary. The psychic being always has an influence on
the thoughts and actions, but one is rarely conscious of it. To
become conscious of the psychic being, one must want to do
so, make one's mind as silent as possible, and enter deep into
the heart of one's being, beyond sensations and thoughts. One
must form the habit of silent concentration and descent into

the depths of one's being.

The discovery of the psychic being is a definite and very concrete fact, as all who have had the experience know.[46]

*

Once the being has entered into contact with the psychic, why does the psychic again hide itself?

It is not the psychic that hides itself, it is the being which returns to its ordinary consciousness!...

It is difficult for it to remain at its highest. One slides down, falls back. Only, the second time the discovery is easier. And each time the road is easier until one no longer falls back.[47]

*

Once the psychic has come to the front, can it withdraw again?

Yes. Generally one has a series of experiences of identification, very intense at first, which later gradually diminish, and then one day you find that they have disappeared. Still you must not be disturbed, for it is quite a common phenomenon. But next time — the second time — the contact is more easily obtained. And then comes a moment, which is not very far off, when as soon as one concentrates and aspires, one gets a contact. One may not have the power of keeping it all the time, but can get it at will. Then, from that moment things become very easy. When one feels a difficulty or there is a problem to be solved, when one wants to make progress or there is just a depression to conquer or an obstacle to be overcome or else simply for the joy of identification (for it is an experience that gives a very concrete joy; at the moment of identification one truly feels a very, very great joy), then, at any moment whatever, one may pause, concentrate for a while and aspire, and quite naturally the contact is established and all problems which were to be solved are solved. Simply to concentrate — to sit down and concentrate — to aspire in this way, and the contact is made, so to say, instantaneously.

There comes a time, as I said, when this does not leave you, that is, it is in the depths of the consciousness and supports all that you do, and you never lose the contact. Then many things disappear. For instance, depression is one of these things, discontentment, revolt, fatigue, depression, all these difficulties. And if one makes it a habit to step back, as we say, in one's consciousness and see on the screen of one's psychic consciousness — see all the circumstances, all the events, all the ideas, all the knowledge, everything — at that moment one sees *that* and has an altogether sure guide for everything that one may do. But this, perforce, takes a very long time to come.[48]

*

What is the meaning of "the psychic opening in the physical consciousness"?

... One can find the psychic through each part of the consciousness: you can find a psychic behind the physical... you can enter into contact with the psychic directly through the physical consciousness, directly through the vital consciousness, directly through the mental consciousness. It is not as though you had to cross all the states of being in order to find the psychic. You can enter the psychic without leaving your physical consciousness, through interiorisation, because it is not an ascent or gradation. It is an interiorisation, and this interiorisation can be done without passing through the other states of being, directly. This is what Sri Aurobindo means: you are in the physical consciousness, nothing prevents you from opening this physical consciousness to the psychic consciousness, you don't need to develop vitally or mentally or to return to these states of being in order to enter into contact with the psychic. You can enter directly. The psychic manifests itself directly in your physical without passing through the other states; that's what it means.[49]

*

I think that one gets the psychic consciousness only when the psychic comes to the surface.

Or when one can go deep enough inside to enter into contact with one's psychic being.[50]

*

... very often, when one touches certain parts of the mind which are under the psychic influence and full of light and the joy of that light, or when one touches certain very pure and very high parts of the emotive being which has the most generous, most unselfish emotions, one also has the impression of being in contact with one's soul. But this is not the true soul, it is not the soul in its very essence. These are parts of the being under its influence and manifesting something of it. So, very often people enter into contact with these parts and this gives them illuminations, great joy, revelations, and they feel they have found their soul. But it is only the part of the being under its influence, one part or another.... Exactly what happens is that one touches these things, has experiences, and then it gets veiled, and one wonders, "How is it that I touched my soul and now have fallen back into this state of ignorance and inconscience!" But that's because one had not touched one's soul, one had touched those parts of the being which are under the influence of the soul and manifest something of it, but are not it.

I have already said many times that when one enters consciously into contact with one's soul and the union is established, it is over, it can no longer be undone, it is something permanent, constant, which resists everything, and which, at any moment whatever, if referred to can be found; whereas the other things — one can have very fine experiences, and then it gets veiled again, and one tells oneself, "How does that happen? I saw my soul and now I don't find it any more!" It was not the soul one had seen. And these things are very beautiful and give you very impressive experiences, but this is not the contact with the psychic being itself.

The contact with the psychic being is definitive, and it is about this that I say, when people ask, "Do I have a contact with my psychic being?", "Your question itself proves that you don't have it!"[51]

*

"We are conscious of only an insignificant portion of our being."   — The Mother, *Questions and Answers 1929*

What are these insignificant parts of our being?

Almost all of them.

There are very few things which are not insignificant; all your ordinary reactions, ordinary thoughts, sensations, actions, movements, — all this is very insignificant. It is only at times, when there is a flash of the higher consciousness through the psychic, an opening into something else, a contact with the psychic being (which may last for a second), at that moment, it is not insignificant. Otherwise, all the rest is repeated in millions and millions of copies. Your way of seeing, acting, all your reactions, thoughts, feelings, all that is ordinary. And you believe you are extraordinary, particularly when you are seized by extraordinary sensations and feelings, those that you consider extraordinary — you believe you are lifted higher, nearing something superhuman; but you are quite mistaken. It is nothing but an ordinary state, deplorably ordinary. You must enter deeper, try to see within yourself if you want to find something which is not insignificant.[52]

*

"The nexus between the psychic being and the higher
consciousness is the principal means of the siddhi."

					Sri Aurobindo, *Lights on Yoga*

*Ordinarily is there not a nexus between the psychic being
and the higher consciousness?*

Ordinarily means in the ordinary life? A relation between
the psychic being...

Yes.

It is almost, almost totally unconscious.

In the ordinary life there's not one person in a million who
has a conscious contact with his psychic being, even momen-
tarily. The psychic being may work from within, but so invis-
ibly and unconsciously for the outer being that it is as though
it did not exist. And in most cases, the immense majority,
almost the totality of cases, it's as though it were asleep, not
at all active, in a kind of torpor.

It is only with the sadhana and a very persistent effort that
one succeeds in having a conscious contact with his psychic
being. Naturally, it is possible that there are exceptional cases
— but this is truly exceptional, and they are so few that they
could be counted — where the psychic being is an entirely
formed, liberated being, master of itself, which has chosen to
return to earth in a human body in order to do its work. And
in this case, even if the person doesn't do the sadhana consciously, it is possible that the psychic being is powerful

enough to establish a more or less conscious relation. But these cases are, so to say, unique and are exceptions which confirm the rule.

In almost, almost all cases, a very, very sustained effort is needed to become aware of one's psychic being. Usually it is considered that if one can do it in thirty years one is very lucky — thirty years of sustained effort, I say. It may happen that it's quicker. But this is so rare that immediately one says, "This is not an ordinary human being." That's the case of people who have been considered more or less divine beings and who were great yogis, great initiates.[53]

*

Naturally it is very difficult to establish a constant contact between the most external physical consciousness and the psychic consciousness, and oh! the physical consciousness has plenty of goodwill; it is very regular, it tries a great deal, but it is slow and heavy, it takes long, it is difficult to move it. It does not get tired, but it makes no effort; it goes its way, quietly. It can take centuries to put the external consciousness in contact with the psychic. But for some reason or other, the vital takes a hand in it. A passion seizes it. It wants this contact (for some reason or other, which is not always a spiritual reason), but it wants this contact. It wants it with all its energy, all its strength, all its passion, all its fervour: in three months the thing is done.

So then, take great care of it [the vital]. Treat it with great consideration but never submit to it. For it will drag you into

all kinds of troublesome and untoward experiments; and if
you succeed in convincing it in some way or other, then you
will advance with giant strides on the path.[54]

*

There are two principal things. This, the capacity for enthusiasm which makes one come out of his greater or lesser
inertia in order to throw himself more or less totally into the
thing which rouses him. As for instance, the artist for his art,
the scientist for his science. And in general, every person
who creates or builds has an opening, the opening of a special faculty, a special possibility, creating an enthusiasm in
him. When this is active, something in the being awakens,
and there is a participation of almost the whole being in the
thing done.

There is this. And then there are those who have an innate
faculty of gratitude, those who have an ardent need to respond, respond with warmth, devotion, joy, to something
which they feel like a marvel hidden behind the whole of life,
behind the tiniest little element, the least little event of life,
who feel this sovereign beauty or infinite Grace which is behind all things.

I knew people who had no knowledge, so to say, of anything, who were hardly educated, whose minds were altogether of the ordinary kind, and who had in them this capacity
of gratitude, of warmth, which gives itself, understands and
is thankful.

Well, for them, the contact with the psychic was very
frequent, almost constant and, to the extent that they were

capable of it, conscious — not very conscious but a little — in the sense that they felt that they were carried, helped, up-lifted above themselves.

These two things prepare people the most. They are born with one or the other; and if they take the trouble, it develops gradually, it increases.

We say: the capacity for enthusiasm, something which throws you out of your miserable and mean little ego; and the generous gratitude, the generosity of the gratitude which also flings itself in thanksgiving out of the little ego. These are the two most powerful levers to enter into contact with the Di-vine in one's psychic being. This serves as a link with the psychic being — the surest link.[55]

*

Already future teachers and future students [of Sri Aurobindo International University Centre] are beginning to arrive, some from outside, new to the climate and customs of the country. They are arriving in the Ashram for the first time and know nothing of its life or its customs. Some of them come with a mental aspiration, either to serve or to learn; others come in the hope of doing yoga, of finding the Divine and uniting with Him; finally there are those who want to devote them-selves entirely to the divine work upon earth. All of them come impelled by their psychic being, which wants to lead them towards self-realisation. They come with their psychic in front and ruling their consciousness; they have a psychic contact with people and things. Everything seems beautiful and good to them, their health improves, their consciousness grows more luminous; they feel happy, peaceful and safe; they think that they have reached their utmost possibility of consciousness. This peace and fullness and joy given by the psychic contact they naturally find everywhere, in everything and everybody. It gives an openness towards the true consciousness pervading here and working out everything. So long as the openness is there, the peace, the fullness and the joy remain with their immediate results of progress, health and fitness in the physical, quietness and goodwill in the vital, clear understanding and broadness in the mental and a general feeling of security and satisfaction. But it is difficult for a human being to keep up a constant contact with his psychic. As soon as he settles down and the freshness of the new experience fades away, the old person comes back to the surface with all its habits, preferences, small manias, shortcomings and misunderstandings; the peace is replaced by restlessness, the joy vanishes, the understanding is blinded and the feeling that the place is the same as everywhere else creeps in, because one has become what one was everywhere else. Instead of seeing only what has been accomplished, he becomes aware more and more and almost exclusively of what has yet to be done; he becomes morose and discontented and blames people and things instead of blaming himself. He complains of the lack of comfort, of the unbearable climate, of the unsuitable food that makes his digestion painful. Taking support from Sri Aurobindo's teaching that the body is an indispensable basis for the yoga, that it should not be neglected and that, on the contrary, great care should be given to it, the physical consciousness concentrates almost exclusively on the body and tries to find ways of satisfying it. This is practically impossible, for, with a very few exceptions, the more it is given, the more it demands. Besides, the physical being is ignorant and blind; it is full of false notions, preconceived ideas, prejudices and preferences. Indeed, it cannot deal effectively with the body. Only the psychic consciousness has the knowledge and the insight needed to do the right thing in the right way.

You might well ask, what is the remedy for this state of affairs? For here we are going round in a vicious circle, since the whole trouble comes from drawing away from the psychic and only the psychic can find the solution to the problems. There is consequently only one remedy: be on your guard, hold fast to the psychic, do not allow anything in your consciousness to slip in between your psychic and yourself, close your ears and your understanding to all other suggestions and rely only on the psychic.

Usually, those who become conscious of their psychic being expect that it will liberate them from vital and physical attractions and activities; they seek to escape from the world in order to live in the joy of contemplation of the Divine, and in the immutable peace of constant contact with Him. The attitude of those who want to practise Sri Aurobindo's integral yoga is quite different. When they have found their psychic being and are united with it, they ask it to turn its gaze towards the physical being in order to act on it with the knowledge that comes from the contact with the Divine, and to transform the body so that it may be able to receive and manifest the divine consciousness and harmony....

So, to all those who come to join the University Centre, I shall say once more: never forget our programme and the deeper reason of your coming here. And if in spite of all your efforts the horizon sometimes darkens, if hope and joy fade away, if enthusiasm flags, remember that it is a sign that you have drawn away from your psychic being and lost contact with its ideal. In this way you will avoid making the mistake of throwing the blame on the people and things around you and thus quite needlessly increasing your sufferings and your difficulties.[56]

*

In the human consciousness everything is *very slow*. When we compare the time that is necessary to realise something with the average length of human existence, it seems interminable. But happily there comes a time when one escapes from this notion, when one begins to feel no longer according to human measures. As soon as one is truly in touch with the psychic, one loses this kind of narrowness and of agony also, this agony which is *so* bad: "I must be quick, I must be quick, there is not much time, I must hurry, there is not much time." One does things very badly or doesn't do them at all any more. But as soon as there is a contact with the psychic, then indeed this disappears; one begins to be a little more vast and calm and peaceful, and to live in eternity.[57]

*

Mother, the psychic being in us is always in contact with the Divine: so one should have this experience all the time, for...

If one were in contact with one's psychic being all the time, yes. But it is a fact: from the moment one is in contact with one's psychic being all the time, one is in contact with the divine Presence all the time. And you may reverse the statement and say, "I shall know that I am in contact with my psychic being all the time, when I am in contact with the divine Presence all the time, in all things. This will be a proof for me that I am in contact with my psychic being."[58]

*

Can it be said that the psychic vibration is the vibration of Divine Love?

Each one of you should be able to get into touch with your own psychic being, it is not an inaccessible thing. Your psychic being is there precisely to put you in contact with the divine forces. And if you are in contact with your psychic being, you begin to feel, to have a kind of perception of what Divine Love can be. As I have just said, it is not enough that one morning you wake up saying, "Oh! I would like to be in contact with Divine Love", it is not like that. If, through a sustained effort, a deep concentration, a great forgetfulness of self, you succeed in coming into touch with your psychic being, you will never dream of thinking, "Oh! I would like to be in contact with Divine Love" — you are in a state in which everything appears to you to be this Divine Love and nothing else.

... So, Divine Love need not be sought and known apart from the psychic being?

No, find your psychic being and you will understand what Divine Love is. Do not try to come into direct contact with Divine Love because this will yet again be a vital desire pushing you; you will perhaps not be aware of it, but it will be a vital desire.

You must make an effort to come into touch with your psychic being, to become aware and free in the consciousness of your psychic being, and then, quite naturally, spontaneously, you will know what Divine Love is.[59]

*

This morning during pranam I was sitting in the pranam room. Sweet and humble tears began to flow; there were intense and ardent prayers. Love and joy were also there. What happiness! What is this movement?

It is a contact established with the psychic, the true soul.[60]

*

I must have felt something during my pranam, because afterwards I wept. O my sweet Mother, why?

Because during the pranam I reestablished the contact between your ordinary consciousness and the psychic consciousness.

The extreme sweetness of the psychic consciousness always makes the outer consciousness weep with emotion.[61]

*

I have known people who were extremely stupid, truly stupid; well, these people succeeded through aspiration — an aspiration which was not formulated, had not even the power to express itself in words — succeeded in coming into contact with their psychic being. It was not a constant contact, it was momentary, at times very fugitive. But while they were in contact with their psychic being, they became remarkably intelligent, they said wonderful things. I knew a girl who had no education, nothing, truly stupid; people said, "There is nothing to be done about it, it is not possible." Well, when she was in contact with her psychic being, she understood the profoundest things and made astounding remarks. But when the contact stopped she became stupid once again. It was not something permanent, it was only the contact that took away her stupidity. So, it is a difficult cure, that is, one must establish the contact with one's psychic being and keep it always.[62]

*

There is a kind of inner communion with the psychic being which takes place when one willingly gives up a desire, and because of this one feels a much greater joy than if one had satisfied his desire.[63]

*

… the first contact with the force gives the psychic being the power to dominate the consciousness and govern the being. But gradually the other parts (mental, vital and physical)

revert to their old activities and the good condition gets
veiled. You must have a persistent will to regain it.[64]

*

... this faith, this trust in the divine Grace is in the psychic
— behind, there, like that, in the psychic, always there. So
sometimes it is the feeling, sometimes it is the thought,
sometimes even it is the body which is in contact with the
psychic, under the influence of the psychic even without
knowing it; and at that moment this kind of trust, of faith
comes in front like that and supports. This happens when
one has momentary contacts with his psychic. For example,
when you find yourself in a very great difficulty or a very
great physical danger, and suddenly feel this, this force coming into you, the force of a faith, an absolute trust in the divine Grace which helps you. So it means that there is a
conscious contact with one's psychic and it comes to help
you — it is a special grace bestowed.... That is, according to
the part which is active or according to the necessity of the
moment, it is here or there or there that suddenly you feel
this trust which takes possession of you and guards you.[65]

*

... the day an external being (physical, mental, vital) enters
into direct and constant contact with the psychic being, one
may say in the same way that the *physical* being of this person is organised by the central divine consciousness. The
moment you put yourself in contact with it, submit yourself

to it, you are organised by it, by the central divine consciousness....[66]

*

It is usually the first contact with the psychic being which brings this experience [reversal of consciousness], but it is only partial, only that *part* of the consciousness — or of the activity in any part of the being — that part of the consciousness which is united with the psychic has the experience. And so, at the moment of that experience, the position of that part of the consciousness, in relation to the other parts and to the world, is completely reversed, it is different. And that is never undone. And if you have the will or take care or are able to put into contact with this part all the problems of your life and all the activities of your being, all the elements of your consciousness, then they begin to be organised in such a way that your being becomes one unity — a single multiplicity, a multiple unity — complex, but organised and centralised around a fixed point, so well that the central will or central consciousness or central truth has the power to govern *all* the parts, for they are all in order, organised around this central Presence.

It seems to me impossible to escape from this necessity if one wants to be and is to be a conscious instrument of the divine Force. You may be moved, pushed into action and used as *unconscious* instruments by the divine Force, if you have a minimum of goodwill and sincerity. But to become a conscious instrument, capable of identification and conscious, willed movements, you must have this inner organisation;

otherwise you will always be running into a chaos somewhere, a confusion somewhere or an obscurity, an unconsciousness somewhere. And naturally your action, even
though guided exclusively by the Divine, will not have the
perfection of expression it has when one has acquired a conscious organisation around this divine Centre.[67]

*

How is it possible to remember one's past lives?

It is through contact with the psychic that one gets fragmen-
tary memories of past lives — the memory of events in which
the psychic took part.

This happens spontaneously when these same elements of
the psychic become active again.

Any deliberate mental effort is liable to produce misleading imaginations.[68]

*

On the psychic plane is there a past, present and future?

In the psychic? Yes, you have even the consciousness of all
the lives you have lived. When you enter into contact with
the psychic you become conscious of all the lives you have
lived, it keeps the absolutely living memory of all the events
in which the psychic took part — not the whole life, not that
one can tell little stories to oneself: that first one was a mon-
key and then later something a little higher, and so on, the

cave-man... no, no stories like that. But all the events of former lives in which the psychic participated are preserved, and when one enters into conscious contact with his psychic being this can be called up like a sort of cinema. But it has no continuity except in lives in which the psychic is absolutely conscious, active, permanently active, that is, constantly associated with the consciousness; so naturally, being constantly associated with the consciousness, it consciously remembers everything that has happened in the real life of the person, and the memories — when one follows these things — the memories of his psychic being are more and more co-ordinated and closer and closer to what could be a physical memory if there were one, in any case of all the intellectual and emotional elements of life, and of some physical events when it was possible for this being to manifest in the outer consciousness; then, at these moments, the whole set of physical circumstances in which one was is kept absolutely intact in the consciousness.[69]

4.

And the moment you are in your psychic being, you have that feeling [looking at death without fear], spontaneously, effortlessly. You soar above the physical life and have the sense of immortality. As for me, I consider this the best remedy [for overcoming fear of death].... This is a deep experience and you can always get it back as soon as you recover the contact with your psychic being. This is a truly interesting phenomenon, for it is automatic. The moment you are in contact with your psychic being, you have the feeling of immortality, of having always been and being always, eternally. And then what comes and goes — these are life's accidents, they have no importance.[70]

*

It is not the psychic being that suffers for personal reasons, it is the mind, the vital and the ordinary consciousness of ignorant man. This is because the contact between the outer consciousness and the psychic consciousness is not well established. He in whom the contact has been well established is always happy.[71]

GROWTH OF THE PSYCHIC BEING

I thought that the soul was perfect in its nature. I don't understand "the ascension of the soul towards the truth from which it springs".

The essence of the soul is divine, but the soul (the psychic being) grows through all the forms of evolution; it becomes more and more individualised and increasingly conscious of itself and its origin.[72] — THE MOTHER

*

Does the psychic being always progress?

There are in the psychic being two very different kinds of progress: one consisting in its formation, building and organisation. For the psychic starts by being only a kind of tiny divine spark within the being and out of this spark will emerge progressively an independent conscious being having its own action and will. The psychic being at its origin is only a spark of the divine consciousness and it is through successive lives that it builds up a conscious individuality. It is a progress similar to that of a growing child. It is a thing in the making. For a long time, in most human beings the psychic is a being in the making. It is not a fully individualised, fully conscious being and master of itself and it needs all its rebirths, one after another, in order to build itself and become fully conscious.

But this sort of progress has an end. There comes a time when the being is fully developed, fully individualised, fully master of itself and its destiny. When this being or one of these psychic beings has reached that stage and takes birth in a human being, that makes a very great difference: the human being, so to say, is born free. He is not tied to circumstances, to surroundings, to his origin and atavism, like ordinary people. He comes into the world with the purpose of doing something, with a work to carry out, a mission to fulfil. From this point of view his progress in growth has come to an end, that is, it is not indispensable for him to take birth again in a body. Till then rebirth is a necessity, for it is through rebirth that he grows; it is in the physical life and in a physical body that he gradually develops and becomes a fully conscious being. But once he is fully formed, he is free, in this sense that he can take birth or not, at will. So there, one kind of progress stops.

But if this fully formed being wants to become an instrument of work for the Divine, if instead of retiring to repose in a psychic bliss, in its own domain, he chooses to be a worker upon earth to help in the fulfilment of the Divine Work, then he has a fresh progress to make, a progress in the capacity for work, for organisation of his work and for expression of the Divine Will. So there is a time when the thing changes. So long as he remains in the world, so long as he chooses to work for the Divine, he will progress. Only if he withdraws into the psychic world and refuses to continue doing the Divine Work or renounces it, can he remain in a static condition outside all progress, because, as I have told you, only upon earth is there progress, only in the physical world; it is not acquired everywhere. In the psychic world there is a kind of blissful repose. One remains what one is, without any movement.[73]   — THE MOTHER

*

In this progression [of the soul] the psychic entity is still veiled, even in man the conscious mental being, by its instruments, by mind and life and body; it is unable to manifest fully, held back from coming to the front where it can stand out as the master of its nature, obliged to submit to a certain determination by the instruments, to a domination of Purusha by Prakriti. But in man the psychic part of the personality is able to develop with a much greater rapidity than in the inferior creation, and a time can arrive when the soul-entity is close to the point at which it will emerge from behind the veil into the open and become the master of its instrumentation in Nature. But this will mean that the secret indwelling spirit, the Daemon, the Godhead within is on the point of emergence; and, when it emerges, it can hardly be doubted that its demand will be, as indeed it already is in the Mind itself when it undergoes the inner psychic influence, for a diviner, a more spiritual existence.[74]   — SRI AUROBINDO

*

... till the self-giving is firmly psychic there will be disturbances, the interval of dark moments between bright ones.

It is only the psychic that keeps on progressing in an unbroken line, its movement a continuous ascension.[75]

THE MOTHER

*

Then everybody is progressing, always, isn't that so?

In a certain way, yes. Only it may not be apparent in one lifetime, because when there is no conscious participation of the being, the movement is relatively slow, even relative to the short duration of human life. And so it is quite possible, for example, that at the moment of death a being seems not to have progressed, and even sometimes it seems to have been going backwards, to have lost what it had at the beginning of its life. But if we take the great life-curve of its psychic being through many lives, there is always a progress. Each experience it had in one of its physical lifetimes helps it to make some progress. But it is the psychic being which always progresses.[76]   — THE MOTHER

*

... if a constant development of being by a developing cosmic experience is the meaning and the building of a new personality in a new birth is the method, then any persistent or complete memory of the past life or lives might be a chain and a serious obstacle: it would be a force for prolonging the old temperament, character, preoccupations, and a tremendous burden hampering the free development of the new personality and its formulation of new experience. A clear and detailed memory of past lives, hatreds, rancours, attachments, connections would be equally a stupendous inconvenience; for it would bind the reborn being to a useless repetition or a compulsory continuation of his surface past and stand heavily in the way of his bringing out new possibilities from the depths of the spirit. If, indeed, a mental learning of things were the heart of the matter, if that were the process of our development, memory would have a great importance; but what happens is a growth of the soul-personality and a growth of the nature by an assimilation into our substance of being, a creative and effective absorption of the essential results of past energies; in this process conscious memory is of no importance. As the tree grows by a subconscient or inconscient assimilation of action of sun and rain and wind and absorption of earth-elements, so the being grows by a subliminal or intraconscient assimilation and absorption of its results of past becoming and an output of potentialities of future becoming.[77]   — SRI AUROBINDO

*

Let us take a divine spark which, through attraction, through affinity and selection, gathers around it a beginning of psychic consciousness (this work is already very perceptible in animals — don't think you are exceptional beings, that you alone have a psychic being and the rest of creation hasn't. It begins in the mineral, it is a little more developed in the plant, and in the animal there is a first glimmer of the psychic presence). Then there comes a moment when this psychic being

is sufficiently developed to have an independent consciousness and a personal will. And then after innumerable lives
more or less individualised, it becomes conscious of itself,
of its movements and of the environment it has chosen for its
growth. Arriving at a certain state of perception, it decides
— generally at the last minute of the life it has just finished
upon earth — the conditions in which its next life will be
passed. Here I must tell you a very important thing: the psychic being can progress and form itself only in the physical
life and upon earth. As soon as it leaves a body, it enters into
a rest which lasts for a more or less long time according to
its own choice and its degree of development — a rest for
assimilation, for a passive progress so to say, a rest for passive growth which will allow this same psychic being to pass
on to new experiences and make a more active progress. But
after having finished one life (which usually ends only when
it has done what it wanted to do), it will have chosen the
environment where it will be born, the approximate place
where it will be born, the conditions and the kind of life in
which it will be born, and a very precise programme of the
experiences through which it will have to pass to be able to
make the progress it wants to make.[78]   — THE MOTHER

*

In what does a psychic being's progress consist?

Individualisation, the capacity to take up all experiences and
organise them around the divine centre.

The aim of the psychic being is to form an individual

being, individualised, "personalised" around the divine centre. Normally, all the experiences of the external life (unless
one does yoga and becomes conscious) pass without organising the inner being, while the psychic being organises these
experiences serially. It wants to realise a particular attitude
towards the Divine. Hence it looks for all favourable experiences in order to have the complete series of opportunities,
so to say, which will allow it to realise this attitude towards
the Divine. Take someone, for example, who wants to have
the experience of nobility — a nobility which makes it impossible for you to act like an ordinary person, which infuses
into you a bravery, a courage which may almost be taken for
rashness because the attitude, the experience demands that
you face danger without showing the least fear. I was telling
you a while ago that I would explain to you what one could
acquire by entering into the body of a king. A king is an ordinary man, isn't he, like all others; he does not have a special
consciousness, but through the necessities of his life, because
he is a kind of symbol to his people, there are things he is
obliged to do which he could never do if he were an ordinary
man. I know this by experience, but I saw this also while looking at photographs which represented a king in actual circumstances: something had happened, which might have been an
attempt on his life, but was averted. The photographs showed
the king inspecting a regiment; all of a sudden someone had
rushed forward, perhaps with a bad intention, perhaps not, for
nothing had happened; in any case, the king had remained completely impassive, absolutely calm, the same smile on his lips,
without moving the least from the place where he was; and he
was quite within sight, an easy target for one who wanted to

rush forward and hurt him. For all I know, this king was not a hero, but because he was a king, he could not take to flight! That would have been ignoble. So he remained calm, without stirring, without showing any outward fear. This is an example of what one can learn in the life of a king.

There is also a true story about Queen Elizabeth. She had come to the last days of her life and was extremely ill. But there was trouble in the country and, about questions of taxation, a group of people (merchants, I believe) had formed a delegation to present a petition to her in the name of a party of the people. She lay very ill in her room, so ill that she could hardly stand. But she got up and dressed to receive them. The lady who was attending upon her cried out, "But it is impossible, you will die of this!" The queen answered quietly, "We shall die afterwards". This is an example from a whole series of experiences one can have in the life of a king, and it is this which justifies the choice of the psychic being when it takes up this kind of life.[79]   — THE MOTHER

*

Mother, since in each new life the mind and vital as well as the body are new, how can the experiences of past lives be useful for them? Do we have to go through all the experiences once again?

That depends on people!

It is not the mind and vital which develop and progress from life to life — except in altogether exceptional cases and at a very advanced stage of evolution — it is the psychic. So, this is what happens: the psychic has alternate periods of activity and rest; it has a life of progress resulting from experiences of the physical life, of active life in a physical body, with all the experiences of the body, the vital and the mind; then, normally, the psychic goes into a kind of rest for assimilation where the result of the progress accomplished during its active existence is worked out, and when this assimilation is finished, when it has absorbed the progress it had prepared in its active life on earth, it comes down again in a new body bringing with it the result of all its progress and, at an advanced stage, it even chooses the environment and the kind of body and the kind of life in which it will live to complete its experience concerning one point or another. In some very advanced cases the psychic can, before leaving the body, decide what kind of life it will have in its next incarnation.

When it has become an almost completely formed and already very conscious being, it presides over the formation of the new body, and usually through an inner influence it chooses the elements and the substance which will form its body in such a way that the body is adapted to the needs of its new experience. But this is at a rather advanced stage. And later, when it is fully formed and returns to earth with the idea of service, of collective help and participation in the divine Work, then it is able to bring to the body in formation certain elements of the mind and vital from previous lives which, having been organised and impregnated with psychic forces in previous lives, could be preserved and, consequently, can participate in the general progress. But this is at a very, very advanced stage.

When the psychic is fully developed and very conscious,

when it becomes a conscious instrument of the divine Will, it organises the vital and the mind in such a way that they too participate in the general harmony and can be preserved.

A high degree of development allows at least some parts of the mental and vital beings to be preserved in spite of the dissolution of the body. If, for instance, some parts — mental or vital — of the human activity have been particularly developed, these elements of the mind and vital are maintained even "in their form" — in the form of the activity which has been fully organised — as, for example, in highly intellectual people who have particularly developed their brains, the mental part of their being keeps this structure and is preserved in the form of an organised brain which has its own life and can be kept unchanged until a future life so as to participate in it with all its gains.

In artists, as for instance in certain musicians who have used their hands in a particularly conscious way, the vital and mental substance is preserved in the form of hands, and these hands remain fully conscious, they can even use the body of living people if there is a special affinity — and so on.

Otherwise, in ordinary people in whom the psychic form is not fully developed and organised, when the psychic leaves the body, the mental and vital forms may persist for a certain time if the death has been particularly peaceful and concentrated, but if a man dies suddenly and in a state of passion, with numerous attachments, well, the different parts of the being are dispersed and live for a shorter or longer time their own life in their own domain, then disappear.

The centre of organisation and transformation is always the presence of the psychic in the body. Therefore, it is a very big mistake to believe that the progress continues or even, as some believe, that it is more complete and rapid in the periods of transition between two physical lives; in general, there is no progress at all, for the psychic enters into a state of rest and the other parts, after a more or less ephemeral life in their own domain, are dissolved.

Earthly life is the place for progress. It is here, on earth, that progress is possible, during the period of earthly existence. And it is the psychic which carries the progress over from one life to another, by organising its own evolution and development itself.[80]   — THE MOTHER

*

When the psychic is about to enter into the world, does it choose in advance the form it is going to take?

It is an interesting question. That depends. As I have just told you [see p. 63], there are psychic beings who are in the making, progressing; these generally, right at the outset, cannot choose much, but when they have arrived at a certain degree of growth and of consciousness (generally while they are still in a physical body and have had a certain amount of experience), they decide at that time what their next field of experience will be like.

I can give you some rather external examples. For instance, a psychic being needed to have the experience of mastery, of power in order to know the reactions and how it is possible to turn all these movements towards the Divine: to learn what a life of power may teach you. It took birth in a king or a queen.

These enjoyed some power and during that time they had their experiences; they reached the end of the field of experience. Now, they know what they wanted to know, they are about to go, they are going to leave their body that's now become useless, and they are going to prepare for the next experience. Well, at that time, when the psychic being is still in the body and has noted what it has learnt, it decides for the next occasion. And sometimes it is a movement of action and reaction: because it has studied one entire field, it needs to study the opposite field. And very often it chooses a very different life from the one it had. So before leaving, it says: "Next time, it is in this domain that I shall take birth...." Suppose, for example, the psychic has reached a stage of growth when it would like to have the chance of working on the physical body to make it capable of coming consciously into contact with the Divine and of transforming it. Now, it is about to leave the body in which it had authority, power, activity, the body it has used for its growth; it says: "Next time I shall take birth in a neutral environment, neither low nor high, where it will not be necessary (how to put it?) to have a highly external life, where one will have neither great power nor great misery — altogether neutral, as you know, the life in between." It chooses that. It returns to its own psychic world for the necessary rest, for assimilation of the experience gained, for preparation of the future experience. It naturally remembers its choice and, before coming down once more, when it has finished its assimilation, when it is time to return, to come down upon earth, it cannot, from that domain, see material things as we see them, you know: they appear to it in another form. But still the differences can be foreseen: the differences of environment, differences of activity in the environment are clearly seen, quite perceptible. It can have a vision that is total or global. It can choose. At times it chooses the country; when it wants a certain kind of education, civilisation, influence, it can choose its country beforehand. Sometimes it can't, sometimes it chooses only its environment and the kind of life it will lead. And then from up there, before it comes down, it looks for the kind of vibrations it wants; it sees them very clearly. It is as though it was aiming at the place where it is going to drop. But it is an approximation because of the fact that another condition is necessary: not only its choice but also a receptivity from below and an aspiration. There must be someone in the environment it has chosen, generally the mother (sometimes both the parents, but the most indispensable is the mother), she must have an aspiration or a receptivity, something sufficiently passive and open or a conscious aspiration towards something higher. And that kindles for the psychic being a little light. In the mass representing for it the environment in which it wants to be born, if under the influence of its own projected will a small light is kindled, then it knows that it is there it must go.

It is necessary, it is this that makes the difference in months or days, perhaps, not so much perhaps in years; however, this creates an uncertainty, and that is why it cannot foretell the exact date: "On that date, that day, at that hour I shall take birth." It needs to find someone receptive. When it sees that, it rushes down. But what happens is something like an image: it is not exactly that, but something very similar. It throws itself down into an unconsciousness, because the physical world, even human consciousness whatever it may be, is very unconscious in comparison with the psychic consciousness. So it rushes into an unconsciousness. It is as though it fell on its head. That stuns it. And so generally, apart from some very very rare exceptions, for a long time it does not know. It does not know any longer where it is nor what it is doing nor why it is there, nothing at all. It finds a great difficulty in express- ing itself, especially through a baby that has no brain, natu- rally; it is only the embryo of a brain which is hardly formed and it does not have the elements for manifesting itself. So it is very rare for a child to manifest immediately the excep- tional being it contains.... That happens. We have heard about such things. It happens, but generally some time is needed. Only slowly it awakens from its stupor and becomes aware that it is there for some reason and by choice. And usually this coincides with the intensive mental education which shuts you completely from the psychic consciousness. So a mass of cir- cumstances, happenings of all kinds, emotions, all sorts of things are necessary to open the inner doors so that one might begin to remember that after all one has come from another world and one has come for a particular reason.

Otherwise, if all went normally, it could very quickly have a connection, very quickly. If it had the luck to find someone possessing a little knowledge, and instead of falling into a world of ignorance, it fell upon a little bit of knowledge, every- thing would be done quite quickly.

But the psychic will and psychic growth escape completely all common notions of justice, of reward and punishment as men understand them. There are religions, there are philoso- phies that tell you all kinds of stories, which are simply the application of notions of human justice to the invisible world, and so these are stupidities. For it is not at all like that truly; the notion of reward and punishment as man understands it is an absurdity. That does not apply at all, not at all to the inner realities. So once you enter the true spiritual world, all that becomes really stupidities. For things are not at all like that.

A large number of people come and tell me: "What then have I done in my previous life to be now in such difficult conditions, with such misfortunes happening to me?" And most often I am obliged to tell them: "But don't you see that it is a blessing upon you, a grace! And perhaps in your previous life you have asked for it so that you could make a greater progress…." These ideas are quite current: "Oh! I am ill. Oh! my body is in a bad condition, what have I done? What crime have I committed in the other life so that in this one…" This is all childishness.[81]   — THE MOTHER

*

Each time that the soul takes birth in a new body it comes with the intention of having a new experience which will help it to develop and to perfect its personality. This is how the psychic being is formed from life to life and becomes a completely conscious and independent personality which, once it has arrived at the summit of its development, is free to choose not only the time of its incarnation, but the place, the purpose and the work to be accomplished.

Its descent into the physical body is necessarily a descent into darkness, ignorance, unconsciousness; and for a very long time it must labour simply to bring a little consciousness into the material substance of the body, before it can make use of it for the experience it has come for. So, if we cultivate the body by a clear-sighted and rational method, at the same time we are helping the growth of the soul, its progress and enlightenment.[82]   — THE MOTHER

*

The soul individualises itself and progressively transforms itself into a psychic being. What are the best conditions for its rapid growth?

It would be more correct to say that the soul puts on a progressive individual form which becomes the psychic being. For since the soul is itself a portion of the Supreme, it is immutable and eternal. The psychic being is progressive and immortal.

All the methods of self-knowledge, self-control and self-mastery are good. You have to choose the one that comes to you spontaneously and best corresponds to your nature. And once having chosen the method, you must use your intelligent will to apply it with an unfailing perseverance that does not shrink from any obstacle, any difficulty. It is a long and minute work which must be undertaken with sincerity and continued with an increasing sincerity ever more scrupulous and integral.

The easy paths generally lead nowhere.[83]   — THE MOTHER

*

How can one make one's psychic personality grow?

It is through all the experiences of life that the psychic personality forms, grows, develops and finally becomes a complete, conscious and free being.

This process of development goes on tirelessly through innumerable lives, and if one is not conscious of it, it is because one is not conscious of one's psychic being — for that is the indispensable starting-point. Through interiorisation and concentration one has to enter into conscious contact with one's psychic being. This psychic being always has an influence on the outer being, but that influence is almost always occult, neither seen nor perceived nor felt, save on truly exceptional occasions.

In order to strengthen the contact and aid, if possible, the development of the conscious psychic personality, one should, while concentrating, turn towards it, aspire to know it and feel it, open oneself to receive its influence, and take great care, each time that one receives an indication from it, to follow it very scrupulously and sincerely. To live in a great aspiration, to take care to become inwardly calm and remain so always as far as possible, to cultivate a perfect sincerity in all the activities of one's being these are the essential conditions for the growth of the psychic being.[84] — THE MOTHER

EMERGENCE OF THE PSYCHIC BEING

Man is a mental being and the mind is the leader of his life and body; but this is a leader who is much led by his followers and has sometimes no other will than what they impose on him. Mind in spite of its power is often impotent before the inconscient and subconscient which obscure its clarity and carry it away on the tide of instinct or impulse; in spite of its clarity it is fooled by vital and emotional suggestions into giving sanction to ignorance and error, to wrong thought and to wrong action, or it is obliged to look on while the nature follows what it knows to be wrong, dangerous or evil. Even when it is strong and clear and dominant, Mind, though it imposes a certain, a considerable mentalised harmony, cannot integrate the whole being and nature. These harmonisations by an inferior control are, besides, inconclusive, because it is one part of the nature which dominates and fulfils itself while the others are coerced and denied their fullness. They can be steps on the way, but not final; therefore in most men there is no such sole dominance and effected partial harmony, but only a predominance and for the rest an unstable equilibrium of a personality half formed, half in formation, sometimes a disequilibrium or unbalance due to the lack of a central government or the disturbance of a formerly achieved partial poise. All must be transitional until a first, though not a final, true harmonisation is achieved by finding our real centre. For the true central being is the soul, but this being stands back and in most human natures is only the secret witness or, one might say, a constitutional ruler who allows his ministers to rule for him, delegates to them his empire, silently assents to their decisions and only now and then puts in a word which they can at any moment override and act otherwise. But this is so long as the soul-personality put forward by the psychic entity is not yet sufficiently developed; when this is strong enough for the inner entity to impose itself through it, then the soul can come forward and control the nature. It is by the coming forward of this true monarch and his taking up of the reins of government that there can take place a real harmonisation of our being and our life.[85]   — SRI AUROBINDO

*

It is true again that it is difficult for man's mind to distinguish entirely the soul or self or any spiritual element in him from the mental and vital formation in which it makes its appearance; but that is only so long as the emergence is not complete. In the animal mind is not quite distinct from its own life-matrix and life-matter; its movements are so involved in the life-movements that it cannot detach itself from them, cannot stand separate and observe them; but in man mind has become separate, he can become aware of his mental operations as distinct from his life-operations, his thought and will can disengage themselves from his sensations and impulses, desires and emotional reactions, can become detached from them, observe and control them, sanction or cancel their functioning: he does not as yet know the secrets of his being well enough to be aware of himself decisively and with certitude as a mental being in a life and body, but he has that impression and can take inwardly that position. So too at first soul in man does not appear as something quite distinct from mind and from mentalised life; its movements are involved in the mind-movements, its operations seem to be mental and emotional activities; the mental human being is not aware of a soul in him standing back from the mind and life and body, detaching itself, seeing and controlling and moulding their action and formation: but, as the inner evolution proceeds, this is precisely what can, must and does happen, — it is the long-delayed but inevitable next step in our evolutionary destiny. There can be a decisive emergence in which the being separates itself from thought and sees itself in an inner silence as the spirit in mind, or separates itself from the life-movements, desires, sensations, kinetic impulses and is aware of itself as the spirit supporting life, or separates itself from the body-sense and knows itself as a spirit ensouling Matter: this is the discovery of ourselves as the Purusha, a mental being or a life-soul or a subtle self supporting the body. This is taken by many as a sufficient discovery of the true self and in a certain sense they are right; for it is the Self or Spirit that so represents itself in regard to the activities of Nature, and this revelation of its presence is enough to disengage the spiritual element: but self-discovery can go farther, it can even put aside all relation to form or action of Nature. For it is seen that these selves are representations of a divine Entity to which mind, life and body are only forms and instruments: we are then the Soul looking at Nature, knowing all her dynamisms in us, not by mental perception and observation, but by an intrinsic consciousness and its direct sense

of things and its intimate exact vision, able therefore by its
emergence to put a close control on our nature and change it.
When there is a complete silence in the being, either a stillness of the whole being or a stillness behind unaffected by
surface movements, then we can become aware of a Self, a
spiritual substance of our being, an existence exceeding even
the soul-individuality, spreading itself into universality, surpassing all dependence on any natural form or action, extending itself upward into a transcendence of which the limits are not visible. It is these liberations of the spiritual part in
us which are the decisive steps of the spiritual evolution in
Nature.

It is only through these decisive movements that the true
character of the evolution becomes evident; for till then there
are only preparatory movements, a pressure of the psychic
Entity on the mind, life and body to develop a true soul-ac-
tion, a pressure of the Spirit or Self for liberation from the
ego, from the surface ignorance, a turning of the mind and
life towards some occult Reality, — preliminary experiences,
partial formulations of a spiritualised mind, a spiritualised
life, but no complete change, no probability of an entire un-
veiling of the soul or self or a radical transformation of the
nature. When there is the decisive emergence, one sign of it
is the status or action in us of an inherent, intrinsic, self-
existent consciousness which knows itself by the mere fact
of being, knows all that is in itself in the same way, by identity with it, begins even to see all that to our mind seems
external in the same manner, by a movement of identity or
by an intrinsic direct consciousness which envelops, pen-
etrates, enters into its object, discovers itself in the object, is

aware in it of something that is not mind or life or body. There is, then, evidently a spiritual consciousness which is other than the mental, and it testifies to the existence of a spiritual being in us which is other than our surface mental personality. But at first this consciousness may confine itself to a status of being separate from the action of our ignorant surface nature, observing it, limiting itself to knowledge, to a seeing of things with a spiritual sense and vision of existence. For action it may still depend upon the mental, vital, bodily instruments, or it may allow them to act according to their own nature and itself remain satisfied with self-experience and self-knowledge, with an inner liberation, an eventual freedom: but it may also and usually does exercise a certain authority, governance, influence on thought, life-movement, physical action, a purifying uplifting control compelling them to move in a higher and purer truth of themselves, to obey or be an instrumentation of an influx of some diviner Power or a luminous direction which is not mental but spiritual and can be recognised as having a certain divine character, — the inspiration of a greater Self or the command of the Ruler of all being, the Ishwara. Or the nature may obey the psychic entity's intimations, move in an inner light, follow an inner guidance. This is already a considerable evolution and amounts to a beginning at least of a psychic and spiritual transformation.[86]   — SRI AUROBINDO

*

The psychic, except in a few extraordinary natures, does not get its full chance in the outer consciousness; it needs some kind of Yoga or Sadhana to come by its own and it is as it emerges more and more in front that it gets clear of the mixture. That is to say, its presence becomes directly felt, not only behind and supporting, but filling the frontal consciousness and no longer dependent or dominated by its instruments — mind, vital and body, but dominating them and moulding them into luminosity and teaching them their true action.[87]   — SRI AUROBINDO

*

The soul in itself contains all possible strength, but most of it is held behind the veil and it is what comes forward in the nature that makes the difference. In some people the psychic element is strong and in others weak; in some people the mind is the strongest part and governs, in others the vital is the strongest part and leads or drives. But by sadhana the psychic being can be more and more brought forward till it is dominant and governs the rest. If it were already governing, then the struggles and difficulties of the mind and vital would not at all be severe; for each man in the light of the psychic would see and feel the truth and more and more follow it.[88]

SRI AUROBINDO

*

... it [the psychic being] is behind the veil and its consciousness also; only a little comes out in the mind and vital and physical. When that consciousness is not concealed, when you are aware of your soul (the psychic being), when its feelings

and consciousness are yours, then you have got the consciousness of the psychic being. The feelings and aspirations of the
psychic being are all turned towards truth and right consciousness and the Divine.[89]　　　　　　　　　　— SRI AUROBINDO

*

The psychic being is always there, but is not felt because it is
covered up by the mind and vital; when it is no longer covered up, it is then said to be awake. When it is awake, it begins to take hold of the rest of the being, to influence it and
change it so that all may become the true expression of the
inner soul. It is this change that is called the inner conversion. There can be no conversion without the awakening of
the psychic being.[90]　　　　　　　　　　— SRI AUROBINDO

*

When the psychic being awakens, you grow conscious of
your own soul; you know your self. And you no longer commit the mistake of identifying yourself with the mental or
with the vital being. You do not mistake them for the soul.

　　Secondly, when awakened, the psychic being gives true
bhakti for God or for the Guru. That bhakti is quite different
from mental or vital bhakti.

　　In the mind one may have admiration or appreciation for
the intellectual greatness of the man — or Guru, but it is merely
mental; it does not carry the matter very far. Of course there is
no harm in having that also. But by itself it does not open the
whole of the inner being; it only establishes a mental contact.

The vital bhakti demands and demands. It imposes its own conditions. It surrenders itself to God, but conditionally. It says to God, "You are so great, I worship you, and now satisfy my this desire or that ambition, make me great, make me a great sadhak, a great yogin, etc."

The unillumined mind also surrenders to the Truth, but makes its own conditions. It says to the Truth, "Satisfy my judgment and my opinion"; it demands that the Truth cast itself in the mind's own forms.

The vital being also insists on the Truth to throw itself into its own movement of force. The vital being pulls at the Higher Power and pulls and pulls at the vital being of the Guru.

Both of them (the mental and the vital) have got an *arrière pensée* (mental reservation) in their surrender.

But the psychic being and its bhakti are not like that. Because it is in direct communication with the Divinity behind, it is capable of true bhakti. Psychic bhakti does not make any demand, makes no reservation. It is satisfied with its own existence. The psychic being knows how to obey the Truth in the right way. It gives itself up truly to God or to Guru, and because it can give itself up truly, therefore it can also receive truly.

Thirdly, when the psychic being comes to the surface, it feels sad when the mental or the vital being is making a fool of itself. That sadness is purity offended.

When the mind is playing its own game or when the vital being is carried away by its own impulses, it is the psychic being which says, "I don't want these things; what am I here for after all? I am here for the Truth, I am not here for these things."

Psychic sadness is again different from mental dissatisfaction or vital sadness or physical depression.

If the psychic being is strong, it makes itself felt on the mental or the vital being, and forces them — compels them — to change. But if it is weak, the other parts take advantage of it and use the psychic sadness to their own advantage.

In some cases the psychic being comes up to the surface and upsets the mental or the vital being and throws everything into disorder. But if the mind or the vital being is stronger than the psychic, then it casts only an occasional influence and gradually retires behind. All its cry is in the wilderness; and the mental or the vital being goes on in its own round.

Lastly, the psychic being refuses to be deceived by appearances. It is not carried away by falsehood. It refuses to be depressed by falsehood — nor does it exaggerate the truth. For example, even if everything around says, "There is no God", the psychic being refuses to believe in it. It says, "I know, and I know because I feel."

And because it knows the thing behind, it is not deceived by appearances. It immediately feels the Force.

Also, when the psychic being is awakened, it throws out all the dross from the emotional being and makes it free from sentimentalism or the lower play of emotionalism.

But it does not carry in it the dryness of the mind or the exaggeration of the vital feelings. It gives the just touch to each emotion.[91]   — SRI AUROBINDO

*

The conversion which keeps the consciousness turned towards

the light and makes the right attitude spontaneous and natural and abiding and rejection also spontaneous is the psychic conversion. That is to say, man usually lives in his vital and the body is its instrument and the mind its counsellor and minister (except for the few mental men who live mostly for the things of the mind, but even they are in subjection to the vital in their ordinary movements). The spiritual conversion begins when the soul begins to insist on a deeper life and is complete when the psychic being becomes the basis or the leader of the consciousness and mind and vital and body are led by it and obey it. Of course, if that once happens fully, doubt, depression and despair cannot come any longer, although there may be and are difficulties still. If it is not fully, still fundamentally accomplished, even then these things either do not come or are brief passing clouds on the surface — for there is a rock of support and certitude at the base, which even if partially covered cannot disappear altogether.[92]

SRI AUROBINDO

٭

In using the expression "opening of the psychic" I was thinking not of an ordinary psychic opening producing some amount of psychic (as opposed to vital) love and bhakti, but of what is called the coming in front of the psychic. When that happens one is aware of the psychic being with its simple spontaneous self-giving and feels its increasing direct control (not merely a veiled or half veiled influence) over mind, vital and physical. Especially there is the psychic discernment which at once lights up the thoughts, emotional

movements, vital pushes, physical habits and leaves nothing
there obscure, substituting the right movements for the wrong
ones. It is this that is difficult and rare, more often the discernment is mental and it is the mind that tries to put all in
order. In that case, it is the descent of the higher consciousness through the mind that opens the psychic, instead of the
psychic opening directly.[93]   — SRI AUROBINDO

*

What is meant by [the psychic's] coming to the front is simply this. The psychic ordinarily is deep within. Very few people are aware of their souls — when they speak of their soul,
they usually mean the vital + mental being or else the (false)
soul of desire. The psychic remains behind and acts only
through the mind, vital and physical wherever it can. For this
reason the psychic being except where it is very much developed has only a small and partial, concealed and mixed or
diluted influence on the life of most men. By coming forward is meant that it comes from behind the veil, its presence
is felt already in the waking daily consciousness, its influence fills, dominates, transforms the mind and vital and their
movements, even the physical. One is aware of one's soul,
feels the psychic to be one's true being, the mind and the rest
begin to be only instruments of the inmost within us.[94]

SRI AUROBINDO

*

"To keep the psychic awake and in front": what does "in front" mean?

That is to say, in the forefront of the consciousness, instead of being pushed behind, in a background which is only very rarely seen; to keep it right in front of the consciousness, in the active consciousness.[95] — THE MOTHER

*

How can one know whether the psychic being is in front or not?

... It is not felt, no? You don't feel it? I am not speaking of a small child, for it has no means of control and observation, it lacks the capacity of observation. But then, when one is no longer a baby, doesn't one feel it? It doesn't make a difference?... (*The child nods in assent.*) Ah!... There is not one of you who will dare to tell me that it makes no difference when the psychic is there, when one feels better within oneself, when one is full of light, hope, goodwill, generosity, compassion for the world, and sees life as a field of action, progress, realisation. Doesn't it make a difference from the days when one is bored, grumbling, when everything seems ugly, unpleasant, wicked, when one loves nobody, wants to break everything, gets angry, feels ill at ease, without strength, without energy, without any joy? That makes a difference, doesn't it?[96] — THE MOTHER

*

How can one know that the psychic being is in front?

My child, when it happens, one understands. It is exactly so long as one doesn't understand that it means that it hasn't come. This is like people asking you, "How can I know whether I am in contact with the Divine?" That itself is enough to prove that they are not. For if they are they can no longer ask the question. It is something understood. For the psychic it is the same thing. When the psychic is in front one knows it, and there is no possibility of any doubt. Consequently one no longer asks the question.[97]   — THE MOTHER

*

[The signs of the psychic's coming forward:] A central love, bhakti, surrender, giving everything, a sight within that sees always clearly what is spiritually right or wrong and automatically rejects the latter — a movement of entire consecration and dedication of all in one to the Mother.[98]

SRI AUROBINDO

*

By what signs can one tell that the psychic being has come to the surface?

One feels peaceful and happy, full of trust, full of a deep and true benevolence, and very close to the divine presence.[99]

THE MOTHER

*

When the psychic being comes in front, there is an automatic perception of the true and untrue, the divine and the undivine, the spiritual right and wrong of things, and the false vital and mental movements and attacks are immediately exposed and fall away and can do nothing; gradually the vital and physical as well as the mind get full of this psychic light and truth and sound feeling and purity....[100]   — SRI AUROBINDO

*

Some of these [higher and deeper] experiences can come by an opening of the inner mental and vital being, the inner and larger and subtler mind and heart and life within us, without any full emergence of the soul, the psychic entity, since there too there is a power of direct contact of consciousness: but the experience might then be of a mixed character; for there could be an emergence not only of the subliminal knowledge but of the subliminal ignorance. An insufficient expansion of the being, a limitation by mental idea, by narrow and selective emotion or by the form of the temperament so that there would be only an imperfect self-creation and action and not the free soul-emergence, could easily occur. In the absence of any or of a complete psychic emergence, experiences of certain kinds, experiences of greater knowledge and force, a surpassing of the ordinary limits, might lead to a magnified ego and even bring about instead of an out-flowering of what is divine or spiritual an uprush of the titanic or demoniac, or might call in agencies and powers which, though not of this disastrous type, are of a powerful but inferior cosmic character. But the rule and guidance of the soul brings into all experience the tendency of light, of integration, of harmony and intimate rightness which is native to the psychic essence.[101]

SRI AUROBINDO

*

The psychic being emerges slowly in most men, even after taking up sadhana. There is so much in the mind and vital that has to change and readjust itself before the psychic can be entirely free. One has to wait till the necessary process has gone far enough before it can burst its agelong veil and come in front to control the nature. It is true that nothing can give so much inner happiness and joy—though peace can come by the mental and vital liberation or through the growth of a strong *samatā* in the being.[102]   — SRI AUROBINDO

*

If the secret psychic Person can come forward into the front and, replacing the desire-soul, govern overtly and entirely and not only partially and from behind the veil this outer nature of mind, life and body, then these can be cast into soul images of what is true, right and beautiful and in the end the whole nature can be turned towards the real aim of life, the supreme victory, the ascent into spiritual existence.[103]

SRI AUROBINDO

*

When the psychic is in the front, the sadhana becomes natural and easy and it is only a question of time and natural development. When the mind or the vital or the physical consciousness is on the top, then the sadhana is a *tapasyā* and a struggle.[104]   — SRI AUROBINDO

*

... when the psychic being gets in front and becomes master, there comes in a fundamentally smooth action and although there are difficulties and undulations of movement, these are no longer of an abrupt or dramatic character.[105]

SRI AUROBINDO

*

There is no process for it [getting the psychic in front]. It comes like the other things—you have to aspire for it and it can only happen when you are sufficiently advanced.[106]

SRI AUROBINDO

*

... the ego and the vital with its claims and desires is always the main obstacle to the emergence of the psychic. For they make one live, act, do sadhana even for one's own sake and psychicisation means to live, act and do sadhana for the sake of the Divine.[107]   — SRI AUROBINDO

*

If desire is rejected and no longer governs the thought, feeling or action and there is a steady aspiration of an entirely sincere self-giving, the psychic usually after a time opens of itself.[108]   — SRI AUROBINDO

*

A first condition of the soul's complete emergence is a direct contact in the surface being with the spiritual Reality. Because it comes from that, the psychic element in us turns always towards whatever in phenomenal Nature seems to belong to a higher Reality and can be accepted as its sign and character. At first, it seeks this Reality through the good, the true, the beautiful, through all that is pure and fine and high and noble: but although this touch through outer signs and characters can modify and prepare the nature, it cannot entirely or most inwardly and profoundly change it. For such an inmost change the direct contact with the Reality itself is indispensable since nothing else can so deeply touch the foundations of our being and stir it or cast the nature by its stir into a ferment of transmutation. Mental representations, emotional and dynamic figures have their use and value; Truth, Good and Beauty are in themselves primary and potent figures of the Reality, and even in their forms as seen by the mind, as felt by the heart, as realised in the life can be lines of an ascent: but it is in a spiritual substance and being of them and of itself that That which they represent has to come into our experience.[109]   — SRI AUROBINDO

*

Aspiration, constant and sincere, and the will to turn to the Divine alone are the best means to bring forward the psychic.[110]   — SRI AUROBINDO

*

Devotion and a more and more complete inner consecration are the best way to open the psychic.[111]   — SRI AUROBINDO

*

That [purity] is one of the most important things for the psychic opening....[112]   — SRI AUROBINDO

*

Then only can the psychic being fully open when the sadhak has got rid of the mixture of vital motives with his sadhana and is capable of a simple and sincere self-offering.... If there is any kind of egoistic turn or insincerity of motive, if the yoga is done under a pressure of vital demands, or partly or wholly to satisfy some spiritual or other ambition, pride, vanity or seeking after power, position or influence over others or with any push towards satisfying any vital desire with the help of the yogic force, then the psychic cannot open, or opens only partially or only at times and shuts again because it is veiled by the vital activities; the psychic fire fails in the strangling vital smoke. Also, if the mind takes the leading part in the yoga and puts the inner soul into the background, or if the bhakti or other movements of the sadhana take more of a vital than of a psychic form, there is the same inability. Purity, simple sincerity and the capacity of an unegoistic unmixed self-offering without pretension or demand are the condition of an entire opening of the psychic being.[113]

SRI AUROBINDO

SECTION SIX

PSYCHIC TRANSFORMATION

*(All passages in this Section have been extracted
from the works of Sri Aurobindo.)*

In the psychic transformation there are three main elements:
(1) the opening of the occult inner mind, inner vital, inner
physical, so that one becomes aware of all that lies behind
the surface mind, life and body — (2) the opening of the
psychic being or soul by which it comes forward and governs the mind, life and body turning all to the Divine — (3)
the opening of the whole lower being to the spiritual truth
— this last may be called the psycho-spiritual part of the
change. It is quite possible for the psychic transformation to
take one beyond the individual into the cosmic. Even the
occult opening establishes a connection with the cosmic
mind, cosmic vital, cosmic physical. The psychic realises
the contact with all-existence, the oneness of the Self, the
universal love and other realisations which lead to the cosmic consciousness.

But all that is a result of the opening to the spiritual above
and it comes by an infiltration or reflection of the spiritual
light and truth in mind, life and body. The spiritual transformation proper begins or becomes possible when one rises
above the mind and lives there governing all from above.
Even in the psychic transformation one can rise above by a
sort of going above of the mental, vital, physical being and a
return, but one does not yet live above in the summit con-

sciousness where overmind has its seat with the other planes
that are above the human Mind.

The supramental transformation can only come when the
lid between the lower and higher hemispheres or halves of
existence is removed and the supermind instead of the
overmind becomes the governing power of the existence....[114]

*

The psychic is the first of two transformations necessary —
if you have the psychic transformation it facilitates im-
mensely the other, i.e., the transformation of the ordinary
human into the higher spiritual consciousness — otherwise
one is likely to have either a slow and dull or exciting but
perilous journey....[115]

*

Everything is dangerous in the sadhana or can be, except
the psychic change.[116]

*

This psychic development and the psychic change of mind,
vital and physical consciousness is of the utmost importance
because it makes safe and easy the descent of the higher consciousness and the spiritual transformation without which the
supramental must always remain far distant. Powers etc. have
their place, but a very minor one so long as this is not done.[117]

*

As for experiences, they are all right but the trouble is that they do not seem to change the nature, they only enrich the consciousness — even the realisation, on the mind level, of the Brahman seems to leave the nature almost where it was, except for a few. That is why we insist on the psychic transformation as the first necessity — for that does change the nature — and its chief instrument is bhakti, surrender, etc.[118]

*

Purification and consecration are two great necessities of sadhana. Those who have experiences before purification run a great risk: it is much better to have the heart pure first, for then the way becomes safe. That is why I advocate the psychic change of the nature first — for that means the purification of the heart: the turning of it wholly to the Divine, the subjection of the mind and the vital to the control of the inner being, the soul. Always, when the soul is in front, one gets the right guidance from within as to what is to be done, what avoided, what is the wrong thing or the true thing in thought, feeling, action. But this inner intimation emerges in proportion as the consciousness grows more and more pure.[119]

*

Between psychicisation and spiritualisation there is a difference. The spiritual is the change that descends from above, the psychic is the change that comes from within by the psychic dominating the mind, vital and physical.[120]

*

Psychicisation means the change of the lower nature bringing right vision into the mind, right impulse and feeling into the vital, right movement and habit into the physical — all turned towards the Divine, all based on love, adoration, bhakti....

The spiritual change is the established descent of the peace, light, knowledge, power, bliss from above, the awareness of the Self and the Divine and of a higher cosmic consciousness and the change of the whole consciousness to that.[121]

*

The two feelings are both of them right — they indicate the two necessities of the sadhana. One is to go inward and open fully the connection between the psychic being and the outer nature. The other is to open upward to the Divine Peace, Force, Light, Ananda above, to rise up into it and bring it down into the nature and the body. Neither of these two movements, the psychic and the spiritual, is complete without the other. If the spiritual ascent and descent are not made, the spiritual transformation of the nature cannot happen; if the full psychic opening and connection is not made, the transformation cannot be complete.

There is no incompatibility between the two movements; some begin the psychic first, others the spiritual first, some carry on both together.[122]

*

One can concentrate in any of the three centres which is easiest to the sadhak or gives most result. The power of the concentration in the heart-centre is to open that centre and by the power of aspiration, love, bhakti, surrender remove the veil which covers and conceals the soul and bring forward the soul or psychic being to govern the mind, life and body and turn and open them all fully to the Divine, removing all that is opposed to that turning and opening.

This is what is called in this yoga the psychic transformation. The power of concentration above the head is to bring peace, silence, liberation from the body sense, the identification with mind and life and open the way for the lower (mental, vital, physical) consciousness to rise up to meet the higher consciousness above and for the powers of the higher (spiritual nature) consciousness to descend into mind, life and body. This is what is called in this yoga the spiritual transformation. If one begins with this movement then the Power from above has in its descent to open all the centres (including the lowest centre) and to bring out the psychic being; for until that is done there is likely to be much difficulty and struggle of the lower consciousness obstructing, mixing with or even refusing the Divine Action from above. If the psychic being is once active this struggle and these difficulties can be greatly minimised.

The power of concentration in the eyebrows is to open the centre there, liberate the inner mind and vision and the inner or yogic consciousness and its experiences and powers. From here also one can open upwards and act also in the lower centres; but the danger of this process is that one may get shut up in one's mental spiritual formations and not come out of them into the free and integral spiritual experience and knowledge and integral change of the being and nature.[123]

*

The first thing to be done is the psychic change and until that has progressed sufficiently, supermind is a far-off thing and people need not think of it at all.[124]

*

It is the supramental alone that can transform the material being, but the physical mind and the physical vital can be very much changed by the action of the psychic and of the overmind. The entire change however is made only when there is the supramental influence. But for the present the psychic is the force that may be relied on for the preliminary purification of the lower nature.[125]

 *

As the crust of the outer nature cracks, as the walls of inner separation break down, the inner light gets through, the inner fire burns in the heart, the substance of the nature and the stuff of consciousness refine to a greater subtlety and purity, and the deeper psychic experiences, those which are not solely of an inner mental or inner vital character, become possible in this subtler, purer, finer substance; the soul begins to unveil itself, the psychic personality reaches its full stature. The soul, the psychic entity, then manifests itself as the central being which upholds mind and life and body and supports all the other powers and functions of the Spirit; it takes up its greater function as the guide and ruler of the nature. A guidance, a governance begins from within which exposes every movement to the light of Truth, repels what is false, obscure, opposed to the divine realisation: every region of the being, every nook and corner of it, every movement, formation, direction, inclination of thought, will, emotion, sensation, action, reaction, motive, disposition, propensity, desire, habit of the conscious or subconscious physical, even the most concealed, camouflaged, mute, recondite, is lighted up with the unerring psychic light, their confusions dissipated, their tangles disentangled, their obscurities, deceptions, self-deceptions precisely indicated and removed; all is purified, set right, the whole nature harmonised, modulated in the psychic key, put in spiritual order. This process may be rapid or tardy according to the amount of obscurity and resistance still left in the nature, but it goes on unfalteringly so long as it is not complete. As a final result the whole conscious being is made perfectly apt for spiritual experience of every kind, turned towards spiritual truth of thought, feeling, sense, action, tuned to the right responses, delivered from the darkness and stubbornness of the tamasic inertia, the turbidities and turbulences and impurities of the rajasic passion and restless unharmonised kinetism, the enlightened rigidities and sattwic limitations or poised balancements of constructed equilibrium which are the character of the Ignorance.

This is the first result, but the second is a free inflow of all kinds of spiritual experience, experience of the Self, experience of the Ishwara and the Divine Shakti, experience of cosmic consciousness, a direct touch with cosmic forces and with the occult movements of universal Nature, a psychic sympathy and unity and inner communication and inter-changes of all kinds with other beings and with Nature, illu-minations of the mind by knowledge, illuminations of the heart by love and devotion and spiritual joy and ecstasy, illu-minations of the sense and the body by higher experience, illuminations of dynamic action in the truth and largeness of a purified mind and heart and soul, the certitudes of the di-vine light and guidance, the joy and power of the divine force working in the will and the conduct. These experiences are the result of an opening outward of the inner and inmost be-ing and nature; for then there comes into play the soul's power of unerring inherent consciousness, its vision, its touch on things which is superior to any mental cognition; there is there, native to the psychic consciousness in its pure work-ing, an immediate sense of the world and its beings, a direct inner contact with them and a direct contact with the Self and with the Divine, — a direct knowledge, a direct sight of Truth and of all truths, a direct penetrating spiritual emotion and feeling, a direct intuition of right will and right action, a power to rule and to create an order of the being not by the gropings of the superficial self, but from within, from the inner truth of self and things and the occult realities of Na-ture.

... But all this change and all this experience, though psy-chic and spiritual in essence and character, would still be, in its parts of life-effectuation, on the mental, vital and physical level; its dynamic spiritual outcome[1] would be a flowering

1. The psychic and the spiritual opening with their experiences and

of the soul in mind and life and body, but in act and form it would be circumscribed within the limitations, — however enlarged, uplifted and rarefied, — of an inferior instrumentation. It would be a reflected and modified manifestation of things whose full reality, intensity, largeness, oneness and diversity of truth and power and delight are above us, above mind and therefore above any perfection, within mind's own formula, of the foundations or superstructure of our present nature. A highest spiritual transformation must intervene on the psychic or psycho-spiritual change; the psychic movement inward to the inner being, the Self or Divinity within us, must be completed by an opening upward to a supreme spiritual status or a higher existence. This can be done by our opening into what is above us, by an ascent of consciousness into the ranges of overmind and supramental nature in which the sense of Self and Spirit is ever unveiled and permanent and in which the self-luminous instrumentation of the Self and Spirit is not restricted or divided as in our mind-nature, life-nature, body-nature. This also the psychic change makes possible; for as it opens us to the cosmic consciousness now hidden from us by many walls of limiting individuality, so also it opens us to what is now superconscient to our normal ity because it is hidden from us by the strong, hard and bright lid of mind, — mind constricting, dividing and separative. The lid thins, is slit, breaks asunder or opens and disappears under the pressure of the psycho-spiritual change and the natural urge of the new spiritualised consciousness towards

---

consequences can lead away from life or to a Nirvana; but they are here being considered solely as steps in a transformation of the nature.

that of which it is an expression here. This effectuation of an aperture and its consequences may not at all take place if there is only a partial psychic emergence satisfied with the experience of the Divine Reality in the normal degrees of the spiritualised mind: but if there is any awakening to the existence of these higher supernormal levels, then an aspiration towards them may break the lid or operate a rift in it. This may happen long before the psycho-spiritual change is complete or even before it has well begun or proceeded far, because the psychic personality has become aware and has an eager concentration towards the superconscience. An early illumination from above or a rending of the upper velamen can come as an outcome of aspiration or some inner readiness, or it may even come uncalled for or not called for by any conscious part of the mind, — perhaps by a secret subliminal necessity or by an action or pressure from the higher levels, by something which is felt as the touch of the Divine Being, the touch of the Spirit, — and its results can be exceedingly powerful. But if it is brought about by a premature pressure from below, it can be attended with difficulties and dangers which are absent when the full psychic emergence precedes this first admission to the superior ranges of our spiritual evolution. The choice, however, does not always rest with our will, for the operations of the spiritual evolution in us are very various, and according to the line it has followed will be the turn taken at any critical phase by the action of the Consciousness-Force in its urge towards a higher self-manifestation and formation of our existence.[126]

*

It follows that the psychic and the spiritual transformation must be far advanced, even as complete as may be, before there can be any beginning of the third and consummating supramental change; for it is only by this double transmutation that the self-will of the Ignorance can be totally altered into a spiritual obedience to the remoulding truth and will of the greater Consciousness of the Infinite. A long, difficult stage of constant effort, energism, austerity of the personal will, *tapasyā*, has ordinarily to be traversed before a more decisive stage can be reached in which a state of self-giving of all the being to the Supreme Being and the Supreme Nature can become total and absolute. There has to be a preliminary stage of seeking and effort with a central offering or self-giving of the heart and soul and mind to the Highest and a later mediate stage of total conscious reliance on its greater Power aiding the personal endeavour; that integral reliance again must grow into a final complete abandonment of oneself in every part and every movement to the working of the higher Truth in the nature. The totality of this abandonment can only come if the psychic change has been complete or the spiritual transformation has reached a very high state of achievement. For it implies a giving up by the mind of all its moulds, ideas, mental formations, of all opinion, of all its habits of intellectual observation and judgment to be replaced first by an intuitive and then by an overmind or supramental functioning which inaugurates the action of a direct Truth-Consciousness, Truth-sight, Truth-discernment, a new consciousness which is in all its ways quite foreign to our mind's present nature. There is demanded too a similar giving up by the vital of its cherished desires, emotions, feelings, impulses, grooves of sensation, forceful mechanism of action and reaction to be replaced by a luminous, desireless, free and yet automatically self-determining force, the force of a centralised universal and impersonal knowledge, power, delight of which the life must become an instrument and an epiphany, but of which it has at present no inkling and no sense of its greater joy and strength for fulfilment. Our physical part has to give up its instincts, needs, blind conservative attachments, settled grooves of nature, its doubt and disbelief in all that is beyond itself, its faith in the inevitability of the fixed functionings of the physical mind, the physical life and the body, that they may be replaced by a new power which establishes its own greater law and functioning in form and force of Matter. Even the inconscient and subconscient have to become conscient in us, susceptible to the higher light, no longer obstructive to the fulfilling action of the Consciousness-Force, but more and more a mould and lower basis of the Spirit. These things cannot be done so long as either mind, life or physical consciousness are the leading powers of being or have any dominance. The admission of such a change can only be brought about by a full emergence of the soul and inner being, the dominance of the psychic and spiritual will and a long working of their light and power on the parts of the being, a psychic and spiritual remoulding of the whole nature.

A unification of the entire being by a breaking down of the wall between the inner and outer nature, — a shifting of the position and centration of the consciousness from the outer to the inner self, a firm foundation on this new basis, a habitual action from this inner self and its will and vision and

an opening up of the individual into the cosmic consciousness — is another necessary condition for the supramental
change. It would be chimerical to hope that the supreme Truth-
Consciousness can establish itself in the narrow formulation
of our surface mind and heart and life, however turned towards spirituality. All the inner centres must have burst open
and released into action their capacities; the psychic entity
must be unveiled and in control. If this first change establishing the being in the inner and larger, a Yogic in place of an
ordinary consciousness has not been done, the greater transmutation is impossible. Moreover the individual must have
sufficiently universalised himself, he must have recast his
individual mind in the boundlessness of a cosmic mentality,
enlarged and vivified his individual life into the immediate
sense and direct experience of the dynamic motion of the
universal life, opened up the communications of his body
with the forces of universal Nature, before he can be capable
of a change which transcends the present cosmic formulation and lifts him beyond the lower hemisphere of universality into a consciousness belonging to its spiritual upper hemisphere. Besides he must have already become aware of what
is now to him superconscient; he must be already a being
conscious of the higher spiritual Light, Power, Knowledge,
Ananda, penetrated by its descending influences, new-made
by a spiritual change. It is possible for the spiritual opening
to take place and its action to proceed before the psychic is
far advanced or complete; for the spiritual influence from
above can awaken, assist and complete the psychic transmutation: all that is necessary is that there should be a sufficient
stress of the psychic entity for the spiritual higher overture to

take place. But the third, the supramental change does not admit of any premature descent of the highest Light; for it can only commence when the supramental Force begins to act directly, and this it does not do if the nature is not ready. For there is too great a disparity between the power of the supreme Force and the capacity of the ordinary nature; the inferior nature would either be unable to bear or, bearing, unable to respond and receive or, receiving, unable to assimilate. Till Nature is ready, the supramental Force has to act indirectly; it puts the intermediary powers of Overmind or Intuition in front, or it works through a modification of itself to which the already half-transformed being can be wholly or partially responsive.[127]

APPENDIX

The following passages, extracted from Sri Aurobindo's epic, *Savitri*, are on topics related to the psychic being dealt with in this book — nature and function of the psychic, its action and influence, contact with the psychic, its growth, discovery of the psychic and its freedom, emergence of the psychic and psychic transformation. Page references pertain to the Sri Aurobindo Birth Centenary Library edition of the epic.

This bodily appearance is not all;
The form deceives, the person is a mask;
Hid deep in man celestial powers can dwell.
His fragile ship conveys through the sea of years
An incognito of the Imperishable.
A spirit that is a flame of God abides,
A fiery portion of the Wonderful,
Artist of his own beauty and delight,
Immortal in our mortal poverty.
This sculptor of the forms of the Infinite,
This screened unrecognised Inhabitant,
Initiate of his own veiled mysteries,
Hides in a small dumb seed his cosmic thought.
In the mute strength of the occult Idea
Determining predestined shape and act,
Passenger from life to life, from scale to scale,
Changing his imaged self from form to form,
He regards the icon growing by his gaze
And in the worm foresees the coming god.

Book One, Canto Three, p. 23

A Person persistent through the lapse of worlds,
Although the same for ever in many shapes
By the outward mind unrecognisable,
Assuming names unknown in unknown climes
Imprints through Time upon the earth's worn page
A growing figure of its secret self,
And learns by experience what the spirit knew,
Till it can see its truth alive and God.

Book Two, Canto Fourteen, p. 293

*

A conscious soul in the Inconscient's world,
Hidden behind our thoughts and hopes and dreams,
An indifferent Master signing Nature's acts
Leaves the vicegerent mind a seeming king.
In his floating house upon the sea of Time
The regent sits at work and never rests:
He is a puppet of the dance of Time;
He is driven by the hours, the moment's call
Compels him with the thronging of life's need
And the babel of the voices of the world.

Book Seven, Canto Two, p. 478

*

This seed-self sown in the Indeterminate
Forfeits its glory of divinity,
Concealing the omnipotence of its Force,
Concealing the omniscience of its Soul;

An agent of its own transcendent Will,
It merges knowledge in the inconscient deep;
Accepting error, sorrow, death and pain,
It pays the ransom of the ignorant Night,
Redeeming by its substance Nature's fall.

Book Three, Canto Three, p. 331

*

As a mother feels and shares her children's lives,
She puts forth a small portion of herself,
A being no bigger than the thumb of man
Into a hidden region of the heart
To face the pang and to forget the bliss,
To share the suffering and endure earth's wounds
And labour mid the labour of the stars.
This in us laughs and weeps, suffers the stroke,
Exults in victory, struggles for the crown;
Identified with the mind and body and life,
It takes on itself their anguish and defeat,
Bleeds with Fate's whips and hangs upon the cross,
Yet is the unwounded and immortal self
Supporting the actor in the human scene.
Through this she sends us her glory and her powers,
Pushes to wisdom's heights, through misery's gulfs;
She gives us strength to do our daily task
And sympathy that partakes of others' grief
And the little strength we have to help our race,
We who must fill the role of the universe
Acting itself out in a slight human shape

And on our shoulders carry the struggling world.
This is in us the godhead small and marred;
In this human portion of divinity
She seats the greatness of the Soul in Time
To uplift from light to light, from power to power,
Till on a heavenly peak it stands, a king.
In body weak, in its heart an invincible might,
It climbs stumbling, held up by an unseen hand,
A toiling spirit in a mortal shape.

                                    Book Seven, Canto Five, pp. 526-27

*

Our soul from its mysterious chamber acts;
Its influence pressing on our heart and mind
Pushes them to exceed their mortal selves.
It seeks for Good and Beauty and for God;
We see beyond self's walls our limitless self,
We gaze through our world's glass at half-seen vasts,
We hunt for the Truth behind apparent things.

                                    Book Seven, Canto Two, p. 485

*

In this investiture of fleshly life
A soul that is a spark of God survives
And sometimes it breaks through the sordid screen
And kindles a fire that makes us half-divine.

                                    Book Two, Canto Five, p. 169

*

Thus came his soul's release from Ignorance,
His mind and body's first spiritual change.
A wide God-knowledge poured down from above,
A new world-knowledge broadened from within:
His daily thoughts looked up to the True and One,
His commonest doings welled from an inner Light.
Awakened to the lines that Nature hides,
Attuned to her movements that exceed our ken,
He grew one with a covert universe.
His grasp surprised her mightiest energies' springs;
He spoke with the unknown Guardians of the worlds,
Forms he descried our mortal eyes see not.
His wide eyes bodied viewless entities,
He saw the cosmic forces at their work
And felt the occult impulse behind man's will.
Time's secrets were to him an oft-read book;
The records of the future and the past
Outlined their excerpts on the etheric page.
One and harmonious by the Maker's skill,
The human in him paced with the divine;
His acts betrayed not the interior flame.
This forged the greatness of his front to earth.
A genius heightened in his body's cells
That knew the meaning of his fate-hedged works
Akin to the march of unaccomplished Powers
Beyond life's arc in spirit's immensities.
Apart he lived in his mind's solitude,
A demigod shaping the lives of men:
One soul's ambition lifted up the race;
A Power worked, but none knew whence it came.

The universal strengths were linked with his;
Filling earth's smallness with their boundless breadths,
He drew the energies that transmute an age.
Immeasurable by the common look,
He made great dreams a mould for coming things
And cast his deeds like bronze to front the years.
His walk through Time outstripped the human stride.

Book One, Canto Three, pp. 44-45

*

A stillness absolute, incommunicable,
Meets the sheer self-discovery of the soul;
A wall of stillness shuts it from the world,
A gulf of stillness swallows up the sense
And makes unreal all that mind has known,
All that the labouring senses still would weave
Prolonging an imaged unreality.
Self's vast spiritual silence occupies Space;
Only the Inconceivable is left,
Only the Nameless without space and time:
Abolished is the burdening need of life:
Thought falls from us, we cease from joy and grief;
The ego is dead; we are freed from being and care,
We have done with birth and death and work and fate.
O soul, it is too early to rejoice!
Thou hast reached the boundless silence of the Self,
Thou hast leaped into a glad divine abyss;
But where hast thou thrown Self's mission and Self's power?
On what dead bank on the Eternal's road?

One was within thee who was self and world,
What hast thou done for his purpose in the stars?
Escape brings not the victory and the crown!
Something thou cam'st to do from the Unknown,
But nothing is finished and the world goes on
Because only half God's cosmic work is done.
Only the everlasting No has neared
And stared into thy eyes and killed thy heart:
But where is the Lover's everlasting Yes,
And immortality in the secret heart,
The voice that chants to the creator Fire,
The symbolled OM, the great assenting Word,
The bridge between the rapture and the calm,
The passion and the beauty of the Bride,
The chamber where the glorious enemies kiss,
The smile that saves, the golden peak of things?
This too is Truth at the mystic fount of Life.
A black veil has been lifted; we have seen
The mighty shadow of the omniscient Lord;
But who has lifted up the veil of light
And who has seen the body of the King?
The mystery of God's birth and acts remains
Leaving unbroken the last chapter's seal,
Unsolved the riddle of the unfinished Play;
The cosmic Player laughs within his mask,
And still the last inviolate secret hides
Behind the human glory of a Form,
Behind the gold eidolon of a Name.
A large white line has figured as a goal,
But far beyond the ineffable suntracks blaze:

What seemed the source and end was a wide gate,
A last bare step into eternity.
An eye has opened upon timelessness,
Infinity takes back the forms it gave,
And through God's darkness or his naked light
His million rays return into the Sun.
There is a zero sign of the Supreme;
Nature left nude and still uncovers God.
But in her grandiose nothingness all is there:
When her strong garbs are torn away from us,
The soul's ignorance is slain but not the soul:
The zero covers an immortal face.
A high and blank negation is not all,
A huge extinction is not God's last word,
Life's ultimate sense, the close of being's course,
The meaning of this great mysterious world.
In absolute silence sleeps an absolute Power.
Awaking, it can wake the trance-bound soul
And in the ray reveal the parent sun:
It can make the world a vessel of Spirit's force,
It can fashion in the clay God's perfect shape.
To free the self is but one radiant pace;
Here to fulfil himself was God's desire.

                                   Book Three, Canto Two, pp. 310-12

*

Earth must transform herself and equal Heaven
Or Heaven descend into earth's mortal state.
But for such vast spiritual change to be,

Out of the mystic cavern in man's heart
The heavenly Psyche must put off her veil
And step into common nature's crowded rooms
And stand uncovered in that nature's front
And rule its thoughts and fill the body and life.

                        Book Seven, Canto Two, pp. 486-87

*

A secret soul behind supporting all
Is master and witness of our ignorant life,
Admits the Person's look and Nature's role.
But once the hidden doors are flung apart
Then the veiled king steps out in Nature's front;
A Light comes down into the Ignorance,
Its heavy painful knot loosens its grasp:
The mind becomes a mastered instrument
And life a hue and figure of the soul.
All happily grows towards knowledge and towards bliss.
A divine Puissance then takes Nature's place
And pushes the movements of our body and mind;
Possessor of our passionate hopes and dreams,
The beloved despot of our thoughts and acts,
She streams into us with her unbound force,
Into mortal limbs the Immortal's rapture and power.
An inner law of beauty shapes our lives;
Our words become the natural speech of Truth,
Each thought is a ripple on a sea of Light.
Then sin and virtue leave the cosmic lists;
They struggle no more in our delivered hearts:

Our acts chime with God's simple natural good
Or serve the rule of a supernal Right.
All moods unlovely, evil and untrue
Forsake their stations in fierce disarray
And hide their shame in the subconscient's dusk.
Then lifts the mind a cry of victory:
"O soul, my soul, we have created Heaven,
Within we have found the kingdom here of God,
His fortress built in a loud ignorant world.
Our life is entrenched between two rivers of Light,
We have turned space into a gulf of peace
And made the body a Capitol of bliss.
What more, what more, if more must still be done?"
In the slow process of the evolving spirit,
In the brief stade between a death and birth
A first perfection's stage is reached at last;
Out of the wood and stone of our nature's stuff
A temple is shaped where the high gods could live.
Even if the struggling world is left outside
One man's perfection still can save the world.
There is won a new proximity to the skies,
A first betrothal of the Earth to Heaven,
A deep concordat between Truth and Life:
A camp of God is pitched in human time.

Book Seven, Canto Five, pp. 530-31

GLOSSARY

anisa — not lord, subject

Ananda — bliss, delight, beatitude, spiritual ecstasy; the essential principle of delight: a self-delight which is the very nature of the transcendent and infinite existence.

Bhakti — devotion, love for the Divine.

central being — the portion of the Divine which supports the individual being and survives from life to life; it has two forms: *jivātman*, which is above the manifestation in life, presiding over it, and the psychic being, which stands behind mind, life and body in the manifestation, supporting them and using them as its instruments.

Consciousness-Force — the Conscious Force that builds the worlds; a universal Energy that is the power of the Cosmic Spirit working out the cosmic and individual truth of things.

Dharma — law; the deepest law of one's nature; the right law of individual and social life; literally, that which one lays hold of and which holds things together.

Higher Mind — *see under* **spiritualised mind.**

inner mind — that which lies behind the surface mind (our ordinary mentality); this inner or subliminal mind senses directly all the things of the mind-plane, is open to the action of a world of mental forces, and can feel their influences which act upon the material world and the life-plane but which at present we can only infer and cannot directly experience.

inner physical — the physical part of the inner being.

inner vital — the vital part of the inner being.

Intuition — *see under* **spiritualised mind**.

Ishwara — Lord, the Divine.

mind (the mental) — "mind" and "mental" connote specially that part of the nature which has to do with cognition and intelligence, with ideas, with mental or thought perceptions, the reactions of thought to things, with the truly mental movements and formations, mental vision and will, etc. that are part of man's intelligence. The ordinary mind has three main parts: mind proper, vital mind, and physical mind.

The **mind proper** is divided into three parts: the thinking mind or intellect, concerned with ideas and knowledge in their own right; the dynamic mind, concerned with the putting out of mental forces for the realisation of the ideas; and the externalising mind, concerned with the expression of ideas in life.

The **vital mind** or desire mind is a mind of dynamic will, action, desire; it is occupied with force and achievement and satisfaction and possession, with enjoyment and suffering, giving and taking, growth and expansion, etc.

The **physical mind** is that part of the mind which is concerned with physical things only; limited by the physical view and experience of things, it mentalises the experience brought by the contact of outward life and things, but does not go beyond that. The mechanical mind, closely connected with the physical mind, goes on repeating without use whatever has happened.

Overtopping the ordinary mind, hidden in our own superconscient parts, there are higher ranges of Mind, gradations of spiritualised mind leading beyond mind to the Supermind. In ascending order they are: Higher Mind, Illumined Mind, Intuition and Overmind.

Nature — the outer or executive side of the Conscious Force which forms and moves the worlds. The higher, divine Nature (Para Prakriti) is free from Ignorance and its consequences; the lower Nature (Apara Prakriti) is a mechanism of active Force put forth for the working of the evolutionary Ignorance. The lower nature of an individual — mind, life and body — are part of Prakriti.

Nirvana — extinction (not necessarily of all being, but of being as we know it, extinction of ego, desire and egoistic action and mentality).

Overmind — *see under* **spiritualised mind.**

the physical (being) — not the body alone, but the whole physical mind, vital, material nature.

physical mind — *see under* **mind**.

Prakriti — Nature; Nature-Force. "Existence is composed of Prakriti and Purusha, the consciousness that sees and the consciousness that executes and formalises what we see. The one we call Soul, the other Nature." (Sri Aurobindo) *see also* **Purusha**.

psyche — the soul; spark of the Divine before it has evolved into an individualised being; the divine essence in the individual. In the course of the evolution, the soul grows and evolves in the form of a soul personality, the psychic being. *See also* **psychic being** *and* **soul**.

the psychic — psychic being, the term is sometimes used for the psyche or soul. *See also* **psyche** *and* **psychic being**.

psychic being — the divine portion in the individual which evolves from life to life, growing, by its experiences until it becomes a fully conscious being. The term "soul" is often used as a synonym for "psychic being", but strictly speaking, the soul is the undifferentiated psychic essence, whereas the psychic being is the individualised soul-personality developed by the psychic essence in the course of evolution. *See also* **the psychic**, **soul**, *and* **soul-personality**.

psychic entity — psychic essence.

psychic essence — the soul in its essence; the divine essence in the individual, the divine spark which supports the evolution of the being in Nature. In the course of the evolution the psychic essence grows and takes form as the psychic being.

psychic personality — *see* **soul-personality**.

psychic principle — psychic essence.

psychicisation — the psychic change in which the psychic being comes forward to dominate the mind, vital and physical so as to change the lower nature.

Purusha — Conscious Being; Conscious-Soul; essential being supporting the play of Prakriti; the Purusha represents the true being on whatever plane it manifests — physical, vital, mental, psychic.

rajasic — of the nature of rajas, the quality of action and passion and struggle impelled by instinct and desire.

sadhana — spiritual practice; the practice of yoga.

sattwic — of the nature of sattwa, the quality of harmony, light, purity and peace.

soul — the psychic essence or entity, the divine essence in the individual; a spark of the Divine that comes down into the manifestation to support the evolution of the individual. In the course of the evolution, the soul grows and evolves in the form of a soul-personality, the psychic being. The term "soul" is also often used as a synonym for "psychic being". *See also* **the psychic** *and* **psychic being**.

soul individuality — *see* **psychic being**.

soul-personality —the psychic being or soul-form developing through evolution and passing from life to life. *See* **psychic being**.

soul-spark — *see* **psyche**.

spiritualised mind, gradations of — higher ranges of mind overtopping our normal mind and leading to Supermind; these successive states, levels or graded powers of being are hidden in our own superconscious parts. In an ascending order the gradations of spiritualised mind are:

Higher Mind: a luminous thought-mind whose instrumentation is through an elevated thought-power and comprehensive mental sight. In the Higher Mind one becomes constantly and closely aware of the Self, the One everywhere and knows and sees habitually with that awareness.

Illumined Mind: a mind no longer of higher thought, but of spiritual light; here the clarity of the intelligence, its tranquil daylight, gives place or subordinates itself to an intense lustre, a splendour and illumination of the Spirit.

Intuition: a power of consciousness nearer and more intimate than the above-mentioned gradations to the original knowlege by identity. What is thought-knowledge in the Higher Mind becomes illumination in the Illumined Mind and direct intimate vision in the Intuition. This true and authentic Intuition must be distinguished from a power of the ordinary mental reason which is too easily confused with it, that power of involved reasoning that reaches its conclusion by a bound and does not need the ordinary steps of the logical mind.

Overmind: The Overmind is a delegate of the Supramental Consciousness, its delegate to the cosmic Ignorance. The Supramental is the total Truth-Consciousness; the Overmind draws down the truths separately and gives them a separate identity.

subliminal — inner, not on the waking surface.

Supermind — the Supramental, the Truth-Consciousness, the Divine Gnosis, the highest divine consciousness and force operative in the universe. A principle of consciousness superior to mentality, it exists, acts and proceeds in the fundamental truth and unity of things and not like the mind in their appearances and phenomenal divisions.

Tapasya (*tapasyā*) — effort, energy, austerity of the personal will; concentration of the will and energy to control the mind, vital and physical and to change them or to bring down the higher consciousness or for any other yogic or high purpose.

transformation — not just a change of consciousness, but the bringing down of the higher, divine consciousness and nature into the lower nature of mind, life and body, and the replacement of the lower by the higher.

true being — *see* **Purusha**.

true mental — *see* **Purusha**.

true physical — *see* **Purusha**.

true vital — *see* **Purusha**.

Truth-Consciousness — *see* **Supermind**.

the vital (being) — the life-nature made up of desires, sensations, feelings, passions, energies of action and of all the play of possessive and other related instincts, such as anger, fear, greed, lust, etc. The vital has three main parts:

higher vital: the mental vital and emotional vital taken together. The mental vital gives a mental expression by thought, speech or otherwise to the emotions, desires, passions, sensations or other movements of the vital being; the emotional vital is the seat of various feelings, such as love, joy, sorrow, hatred and the rest.

central vital or **vital proper**: dynamic, sensational and passionate, it is the seat of the stronger vital longings and reactions, such as ambition, pride, fear, love of fame, attractions and repulsions, desires and passions of various kinds and the field of many vital energies.

lower vital: made up of the smaller movements of human life-desire and life-reactions, it is occupied with small desires and feelings, such as food desire, sexual desire, small likings, dislikings, vanity, quarrels, love of praise, anger at blame, little wishes of all kinds, etc.

REFERENCES

Passages in this book, serially numbered 1-127, have been extracted from the following volumes of the Sri Aurobindo Birth Centenary Library (1970-1973) and the Collected Works of the Mother (1972-1987) published by Sri Aurobindo Ashram, Pondicherry.

Sri Aurobindo Birth Centenary Library (SABCL)

Vol.   Title
15   *Social and Political Thought*
19   *The Life Divine — Book Two Part Two*
20   *The Synthesis of Yoga — Parts One and Two*
21   *The Synthesis of Yoga — Parts Three and Four*
22   *Letters on Yoga — Part One*
23   *Letters on Yoga — Parts Two and Three*
24   *Letters on Yoga — Part Four*

Collected Works of the Mother (CWM)

Vol.   Title
3   *Questions and Answers*
4   *Questions and Answers 1950-51*
5   *Questions and Answers 1953*
6   *Questions and Answers 1954*
7   *Questions and Answers 1955*
8   *Questions and Answers 1956*
9   *Questions and Answers 1957-58*
10   *On Thoughts and Aphorisms*
12   *On Education*
14   *Words of the Mother*
15   *Words of the Mother*
16   *Some Answers from the Mother*
17   *More Answers from the Mother*

References are given below in an abbreviated form. The initial numeral is the serial number of the passage in this book located at the end of each passage. This is followed by the abbreviated title of the series (SABCL or CWM listed on the previous page), followed by the volume number and the page number(s) where the passage occurs. For example:

1. SABCL: 9:364 indicates that passage 1 is to be found in the Sri Aurobindo Birth Centenary Library, Volume 9, p. 364.

The Psychic Being — Its Nature and Function

1. SABCL 9:364
2. SABCL 19:891-93
3. SABCL 22:268-69
4. SABCL 24:1111
5. SABCL 20:145-49
6. CWM 6:27-28
7. CWM 7:105-06
8. CWM 15:323
9. CWM 15:326-27
10. CWM 4:139-40
11. CWM 12:430
12. CWM 3:62-63
13. CWM 3:125
14. SABCL 24:1115
15. SABCL 20:140-41
16. CWM 7:253
17. CWM 7:20
18. SABCL 23:1047
19. CWM 3:130
20. CWM 3:124-25
21. CWM 3:158
22. CWM 2:57
23. CWM 5:394
24. CWM 4:164-65
25. CWM 3:63-64
26. CWM 16:223
27. CWM 14:107-08
28. CWM 6:160-62
29. CWM9:16-17
30. CWM 6:447-48
31. CWM 7:76

Action and Influence of the Psychic Being

32. SABCL 19:893-95
33. CWM 8: 193-94
34. CWM 4:165
35. SABCL 9:362-63
36. SABCL 24:1108
37. SABCL 24:1115
38. CWM 16:248
39. CWM 7:422-23
40. CWM 17:76
41. CWM 6:393, 395
42. CWM 7:222-23
43. CWM 4:261
44. CWM 4:145-46

Contact with the Psychic Being

45. CWM 5:396

46. CWM 16:397
47. CWM 6:24
48. CWM 6:33-34
49. CWM 7:74
50. CWM 17:90
51. CWM 7:263-64
52. CWM 5:1
53. CWM 7:272-73
54. CWM 5:258-59
55. CWM 7:423-24
56. CWM 12:45-47
57. CWM 6:334
58. CWM 6:365-66
59. CWM 4:245-46
60. CWM 17:16
61. CWM 17:61
62. CWM 4:369-70
63. CWM 7:39-40
64. CWM 17:122
65. CWM 7:116-17
66. CWM 4:141
67. CWM 8:174-75
68. CWM 17:371
69. CWM 7:221
70. CWM 5:317
71. CWM 14:357

Growth of the Psychic Being

72. CWM 17:78
73. CWM 5:205-06
74. SABCL 19:844-45
75. CWM 3:124
76. CWM 7:425
77. SABCL 19:818-19
78. CWM 4:143-44

79. CWM 4:149-51
80. CWM 9:268-70
81. CWM 5:215-18
82. CWM 10:29-30
83. CWM 16:248
84. CWM 16:223-24

Emergence of the Psychic Being

85. SABCL 19:899-900
86. SABCL 19:855-56
87. SABCL 9:363
88. SABCL 24:1109-10
89. SABCL 24:1098
90. SABCL 24:1096
91. SABCL 24:1103-04
92. SABCL 24:1105
93. SABCL 24:1096
94. SABCL 24:1097
95. CWM 6:409
96. CWM 6:6
97. CWM 6:396
98. SABCL 24:1104-05
99. CWM 17:74
100. SABCL 24:1107-08
101. SABCL 19:909
102. SABCL 24:1098
103. SABCL 18:226-27
104. SABCL 24:1109
105. SABCL 24:1109
106. SABCL 24:1098
107. SABCL 24:1099
108. SABCL 24:1099
109. SABCL 19:900-01
110. SABCL 24:1099
111. SABCL 24:1099

112. SABCL 25:175
113. SABCL 24:1098-99

Psychic Transformation

114. SABCL 24:1092-93
115. SABCL 24:1094
116. SABCL 24:1095
117. SABCL 24:1095
118. SABCL 24:1609

119. SABCL 24:902-03
120. SABCL 24:1093
121. SABCL 24:1093
122. SABCL 24:1093-94
123. SABCL 23:725
124. SABCL 24:1223
125. SABCL 24:1223-24
126. SABCL 19:907-10
127. SABCL 19:929-31

INDEX

Compilations from the works of
Sri Aurobindo and the Mother
by the same editor

Living Within
The Yoga Approach to
Psychological Health and Growth

The Psychic Being
Soul — Its Nature, Mission and Evolution

The Hidden Forces of Life

Growing Within
The Psychology of Inner Development

Looking from Within
A Seeker's Guide to Attitudes for Mastery and
Inner Growth

Powers Within

Living Words
Soul-Kindlers for the New Millennium

Our Many Selves
Practical Yogic Psychology

Emergence of the Psychic
Governance of Life by the Soul

The Yoga of Sleep and Dreams
The Night-School of Sadhana

The God-Touch
And Other Lights from Sri Aurobindo's *Savitri*

Gifts of Grace
Five Aids for Inner Growth

Steps to Freedom and Mastery

Morality, Idealism, Religion and Yoga
The Meaning of Spirituality